ALAN

"

n "

BARKING
DOGS

taking the gospel to where it's
desperately needed and hardest to find

ANDY RUSHWORTH

malcolm down

PUBLISHING

First published 2017 by Malcolm Down Publishing Ltd.
www.malcolmdown.co.uk

British Library Cataloguing in Publication Data
A catalogue record for this book is available from the British Library.

ISBN 978-1-910786-64-2

Some names have been changed to protect identities

Cover design by Ben Walker
Printed in the UK

Endorsements

'Fresh. Normal. Quirky. Regular. Irregular. Old. Young. Rebellious. Tender. Andy Rushworth is all of these. Plus more. All wrapped up in a lovable, worn, tattooed, lumberjacked exterior that even grannies would fall for. He's a uniter of both personality traits and personality types! He's unique yet regular; 'seen it all' yet sensitive. And he's written a book. It's this book that will get you even if you thought it wouldn't. It's not anti-church, it's just not fond of religion. And it's not anti-rebel, it's just not fond of you staying that way forever. And nor are you. Everyone wants to change for the better. Yet sometimes you just need an Andy to tug at you like your pet terrier and lead you to a different way of thinking and help you reopen your childish wells of believing. He actually believes in you. And really believes in a new you, a fresh you and a better you. *Barking Dogs* may make you a believer in both as well.
Relax. Let Andy take you there. And by the end of the book, if you don't agree, he's still there. Believing. That's what he's like.'
Dave Gilpin
Pastor
Hope City Church

I have known Andy Rushworth for many years. He is a missionary with a real heart of gold. *Barking Dogs* is a great read; you can hear Andy's voice on every page ... chapter eight is both hilarious and inspiring! God is speaking through this book, and I pray that as you read it, He will speak to you.
Revd Canon Mick Woodhead
Team Rector
STC Sheffield, UK

Barking Dogs is a reminder that God's heart beats for us. Andy combines biblical truth with a personal story that shows God's purpose and love for the world around us. This book will start an honest but needed conversation for the Church and for those who have rejected God's plan. Pick it up. Read it. You will not be the same!

Pastor Bob Sandler
AG State Youth Director SC, USA

Andy Rushworth ruined me. His influence meant that I could never view my faith as something only for myself. His passion to win souls from every walk of life imprinted itself on me as a new believer, causing my heart to beat for the lost. Because of him I've always taken for granted that we Christians are all in this for the same reason – to see the broken radically saved and released into a life of purpose. If you're willing to be shaken, the contents of this book will move you beyond your comfort zone and cause you to see the world with new eyes. Because where others see the disaffected and uncivilised, Andy Rushworth sees an army of disciples. His foresight and faith always cause my heart to open a little wider.

Philippa Hanna
International Recording Artist

In the Bible God called Jonah to go to a bunch of people that he thought deserved everything they had coming their way, and didn't deserve to hear any good news. Eventually, Jonah went. In this book Andy tells real-life stories about the unusual places that God had called him to go and share the Good News. Just like God's messengers in the Old Testament and their antics, Andy's stories are unconventional, provocative, and able to challenge what we think we know about God, God's love, and where mercy should be preached. They remind us that wherever we go, we find that God is already at work there.

Revd Harry Steele
Husband, Father, Friend and Twenty-first-century Theologian

Accompany Andy as he reflects on some of his life experiences with humour, poignancy, and a good dose of reality. In doing so, I found some of my personal comfort zones being uncomfortably challenged (not a bad thing on occasion). This is an invitation to join in the reflection, and if appropriate, to then live differently.

David Jones
Senior Leader
City Church (Great Grimsby & NE Lincs)
Director of Ground Level Network, UK

Acknowledgements

Sharron, you are my angel and I thank God every day for blessing my life with you. Thank you for never failing to believe in me. 'If you live to be 100, I hope I live to be 100 minus 1 day, so I never have to live without you' (Winnie the Pooh).

Ben, Beth and Lauren
Thank you for loving me and listening while I read what I have written when we have dinner together... you always give honest feedback.

Grandad (the late Benny Finch)
Thank you for teaching me to have faith, vision and a boldness in God ... You never stopped at the barking dogs.

Mum and Dad
Your unconditional love and support never ceases to inspire me.

Paul Norris
A man most faithful to his call. Thank you for the early years of ministry.

John Ford
A man of faith and patience, you needed both with me.

Phil Cana
Steadfast and strong in the faith. Thank you for standing with me.

Peter Williams
A remarkable man. You lead with passion and your heart loves well. Thank you for the best five years of ministry I have known.

acknowledgements

Mick Woodhead
You are a kingdom builder. Thank you for never losing faith in me … you have taught me more than you know, and your three-word sermon to me several years ago will stay with me all my life: 'Stop Blaming God'.

Ruth, thank you for your editing skills, you sure needed them with me. Ben, you have said in pictures what takes me many words to say. My STC family. Bob Sandler (my Colonial Brother). Neil McCormick (Chicago – one day). Mark (Rock Star) Richardson, a finer record dealer there is not. Mick (You're Half Way to Being Alright), you're the best thing about Mondays. Joe, the years of coming home in the early hours stinking of smoke and beer was all worth it. The Full Monty Boys, Neil, Rob and Jon. Laura (beautiful), Craig and Sarah, Neil and Debs, Jason and Karen. Big Mick (we're all Blades, aren't we), Neil and Fiona, Rachel, Andy (the beard), and last but by no means least, Harry and Zoey Steele.

I am rich for I have known your love.

Contents

Introduction

If the postman stopped at every barking dog,
then the mail would never get delivered.

Think about it!

It's true!

We would never receive our letters, parcels and gifts that are sent to us and delivered by the postman, if the postman didn't find a way to get around the barking dogs.

Being a Christian, I believe I carry the greatest message the world has ever been given... the gospel: that God so loved the world that He gave His one and only Son (Jesus), so that if we believe in Him we would not perish but receive eternal life (see John 3:16).

God has given His letter, His parcel, His gift to every Christian, but we so often let the barking dogs of our lives stop us delivering them.

Been hurt in church?

Are you sick?

Been a victim of crime?

Had a broken marriage?

Don't see much of your kids?

Lack confidence?

Been bankrupt?

Struggle with your self-image?

Outlived your child?

Suffer from depression?

Struggling with being single?

Hooked on porn?

Looking for a fight?

Failed in a business adventure?

Made too many mistakes?

All these dogs can stop us giving away freely the great love that we have received.

There is nothing like receiving a package that you have been waiting for. The day it arrives is a good one, and opening it to find all that you have been waiting for is satisfying.

But at this point let me say 'Thank you' for picking this book up and reading it. I have struggled with confidence in writing it, even with so many people over the years encouraging me. I decided to shut up my barking dogs once and for all.

The following pages are full of my experiences in trying to take 'The Great Love' into the places where it is desperately needed yet hardest to find.

My intentions are not to offend you or the way you do church, but to encourage you to give God's love away freely, just as you have freely received it.

This is my experience, and how God has opened doors for me when I have decided that barking dogs will not stop me delivering His message of love and forgiveness.

If you are ready for a challenge, a great adventure, if you're feeling your Christian walk is... well... a little boring, then let me encourage you to take a deep breath and breathe in God's strength and passion, filling you with His compassion and courage.

We carry God's message, one that everyday people need to hear. At times it's delivered with few or many words and other times it's delivered through a listening ear, a warm embrace or an act of love. But be assured it needs to be delivered and you are the postman/postwoman. The world depends on you, the kingdom needs you. And those around you, wherever they are found, deserve God's love.

My hope is that as you read these pages you too will be encouraged and inspired to take the gospel into the dark places, into the ordinary places, and be amazed at what God can do through you.

A final note to make this journey together more exciting: when you come across a song title, I encourage you to go to iTunes, Spotify or another music source and have a listen. It will help set the scene.

Are you ready?

Come on, let's go...

Contact the author:

dapperwords@icloud.com

HIDDEN TREASURE

Chapter One: Hidden Treasure

Do not store up for yourselves treasures on earth, where
moths and vermin destroy, and where thieves break
in and steal. But store up for yourselves treasures in
heaven, where moths and vermin do not destroy, and
where thieves do not break in and steal. For where your
treasure is, there your heart will be also.
(Matthew 6:19–21)

Whoever has your heart has your life.

In the belly of a whale

Whales are fantastic creatures. Take the Blue Whale, for instance;
it's the largest creature that has ever lived on planet Earth. It can
weigh over 180,000kg and its tongue alone can weigh as much
as an elephant. Their lifespan is between eighty to ninety years
but they have been known to live 110 years. They inhabit all the
world's oceans, spending their summers feeding in polar waters,
and they undertake long migrations towards the equator as winter
arrives.

God is a mastermind at creating.

I remember hearing two stories about whales when I was a kid.

The first story was about whale hunters who caught a sperm whale
which had died of constipation. When the whalers started skinning
the whale they found James Bartley (1870–1909) inside its belly,
still alive. Apparently his boat was attacked by the whale which
then swallowed him.

The original article was written anonymously: 'Man in a Whale's

Stomach/Rescue of a Modern Day Jonah' on page 8 of the 22nd August, 1891 issue of the *Yarmouth Mercury* newspaper of Great Yarmouth, UK. It was said that his skin had been bleached by the gastric juices, and that he was blind for the rest of his life. He actually lived another eighteen years before passing away and being buried in Gloucester.

He had a great story to tell his grandchildren and the fellas down the local pub!

The second story was from the Bible, during a Sunday school class. It was a fantastic story about a man called Jonah.

God had asked Jonah to go and preach His message of love and repentance in a place called Nineveh. Now, Jonah didn't like Nineveh or the people that lived there. It would be like God asking an Englishman to go to France and tell the people there about His 'Great Love'. Although Jonah loved God and wanted to do His will, he couldn't find the love or grace to obey Him, so he hopped onto a boat and sailed away in the opposite direction.

Now, the Bible tells us that the sailors on that boat knew that Jonah was disobeying God. So when an unusual storm hit the sea and their boat, they were convinced that it was sent by God because of Jonah's disobedience.

So they did what any sailor would do and threw overboard what they believed would calm the storm and prevent their ship going down. They must have all thought Jonah would drown in the raging waves, but God sent a giant fish/whale to swallow Jonah.

Can you imagine being swallowed by a whale?

The breath of that whale must have stunk of old fish. Some Sunday school teachers will show you pictures of Jonah inside the belly of that whale, where he is sitting on a chair at a table with a little candle on it, neatly dressed and with a thoughtful look on his face.

It wasn't like that at all: you would only have to have listened to James Bartley's story to know that.

Jonah was in that whale's belly for three days, tightly surrounded by intestines and all the digestive juices that were trying to break him down, in complete darkness.

I believe one of the reasons why God allowed Jonah to experience such a thing was to scar him so much through his disobedience that he would never forget that what he had been through, the people of Nineveh were going through every day of their lives. And that moved God to act upon His great compassion for them.

The people of Nineveh were trapped in the belly of life, a life in which God was ignored and a life that was slowly digesting them, taking all the good out and eventually leaving them broken and feeling like their life was a pile of crap.

God wanted to step into their world and He needed Jonah to introduce Him to them. Now, Jonah had two ways out of that whale. He could change his mind and obey God by going to Nineveh and come out the same way he went in, or he could refuse to go, be digested and eventually come out in a giant whale poo!

Jonah chose to obey God, so God commanded the whale to vomit Jonah up.

When you choose to obey God after disobeying Him, there is a transition that takes place; it's not always an easy one, but you cross over from death to life, from a curse to a blessing, and each step you take, you brush off the vomit of this world.

I believe Jonah was so moved by his experience that he became filled with a great compassion and love for the people of Nineveh, a love that he had never experienced before, and one that would drive him to go and speak the message of God to them with authority and passion. To deliver 'The Great Love'.

There are places all around us that are like the belly of Jonah's whale.

Places that digest humankind, sucking all the good out of them until nothing is left.

Those places have names: they are the townships of Africa, the slums of South America, the housing estates of Europe, the ghettos of America. They are the lonely room when the teenage girl sits sobbing because she is pregnant; they are the kitchens where mums pray for the children who have wandered away from a loving family; they are the car in which a man sits, and believes this world would be better off if he took his own life; they are drugs, sexual acts, and they are any place where broken people are covered in the crap of this life – and the real them, the real treasure that they are, lies buried under the cares and struggles of their world.

Jonah didn't see the people of Nineveh as treasure, he just saw them as a nation, a group of people that he didn't like. But God saw them as sons and daughters who had wandered away from His love and care. He cared for them and couldn't ignore their troubles any longer.

> **I wonder how many Jonahs
> sit in our churches on Sundays?**

...unwilling to go to the places they don't like, or that their boundaries won't allow them to be in.

I wonder how many of them are being digested by their own faith?

One thing I do know: you don't have to look far to find lives that need to hear and experience 'The Great Love'.

Until the need to take 'The Great Love' into the margins becomes greater than the need to attend church on Sunday morning, God's treasure that is humankind will remain buried under the crap of life.

But for those who are compelled by 'The Great Love' in them to go into the forgotten places of our communities (all the world), the joy and relevance of Sunday morning becomes like fresh bread to them.

Friends in low places

I love going to the local pub. It's a place where you meet a variety of characters, hear some of the funniest stories and enjoy the company of people that you would never get to meet unless you went to the local.

Sounds a lot like church – or like the way church could be.

I have two local pubs; there is the one at the top of our road called 'The Prince of Wales' (I think the Prince stayed there many years ago), and there is the one down the road called 'The Broadfield'.

If Sharron and I are going out, I take her to 'The Prince'. It's a nice, clean and cool-looking pub, which serves good food, and you never hear any bad language... not often, anyway.

But if I am going to the local on my own or to meet some guys before we head off to see the mighty Blades (Sheffield United) play at Bramall Lane, then I go to 'The Broady'... it's not as clean, the toilets have a funny herbal smell in them, and the language can get colourful at times... that, mixed with the odd scuffle, all adds up to being a lively place to be for a bloke.

One of the qualities I have tried to nurture in my life these past years is 'self-awareness'.

I have come to learn what makes me mad, sad, what moves me to tears, what inspires me, what disinterests me and what brings me joy.

But I have a confession to make: I am a little puzzled why a particular country song moves me so much when I hear it. I am not a great fan of country music. I once heard someone say if you play country records backwards, you get your house back, girl back, car back and dog back... go on, laugh – you know you want to! ;-)

It's true, country music usually consists of a story about a man who loses everything. I grew up listening to country when travelling with my dad in his car. I have never forgotten some of those songs, and when hearing them today they bring back many fond memories. A few years ago I went to America on a ministry trip and one of the places we were going to was Kalamazoo. Now, that was a big deal for me because my dad used to play a country song in the car about 'Della and the Dealer and a Dog named Jake and a Cat named Kalamazoo'. I never knew it was a real place.

I especially loved Johnny Cash and I still listen to him now all these years later. To me Johnny Cash was the original punk of country music. He said what needed to be said in a way that everyday people appreciated. I can't wait to spend time with him in heaven, with my dad, when we both get there.

I won't ever forget the first time I heard 'Friends in Low Places' by Garth Brooks. For those of you that have never heard of Garth, he is the biggest selling artist in history, outselling the Beatles, Elvis, U2 and Michael Jackson.

The song is about a guy who doesn't fit in with big social occasions, but would rather be at the pub with his friends, where the beer and whisky chases their everyday blues away. Now, I am not condoning excessive drinking or saying that your answer will be found in the bottom of a bottle. But when I hear that song, I am moved to tears.

I know, I know... sounds stupid, but this song stirs my desire to connect with those who will never set foot inside a church for a variety of reasons – they believe Christians are homophobic, hypocritical, boring and judgemental, and love to judge those outside the church doors. But their friends in the bar, the ones they will sit with and have a lot in common with, they don't judge, and in most cases would give you the shirt off their back.

> **Jesus had friends in low places, and He never judged them, but He loved them into a better life.**

I think of the prostitute who poured perfume over His feet, the woman caught in adultery, Zacchaeus the tax man who charged more than he should, the demon-possessed man called Legion, the blind, lame and terminally sick; Jesus spent time with them all... He had friends in low places.

I remember going on a men's mission trip to Honduras in South America while I was living in the States. At the time I was working in a church as a youth pastor and decided to join the men's mission team that was going to a place called La Ceiba to help lay some foundations for a new church building.

The church was very firm about the use of tobacco and the consumption of alcohol, and all the men were under strict instructions not to be partakers in either of them. We all had to sign a contract to say that we wouldn't drink or smoke while on the trip, and that we would not attempt to bring any alcohol or tobacco products home through the duty free.

I struggled with this but signed the contract anyway. The reason why I struggled was that if this was a mission trip, then surely we would want to go into those places that non-Christians went? Bars, pubs etc.? I wanted to make friends and introduce them to Jesus.

Once we arrived in La Ceiba, we checked into our hotel. Well, 'hotel' would have been a fancy name for that place. It was probably one of the dirtiest and roughest hotels I have stayed in. But I just got on with it; after all, this was a mission trip.

Once we got settled in, I noticed that the hotel had a roof-top bar.

The contract we all had signed said nothing about going to bars, just that we couldn't drink alcohol... So, on the second night, I and my good friend and roommate, Wes, decided to go and see what this roof-top bar was like.

As we walked in we noticed it was full of the people that the church had forgotten about, simply because they enjoyed a beer. Now, Wes and I didn't want to break our contract (though it was a hot evening and a cold beer would have gone down a treat), so we devised a plan... We wanted to get in on some of the conversations that people were having, we wanted to make friends, but time was not on our side... so we did something which we thought was very wise... We decided to buy everyone in the bar a drink! ☺ Everyone loves a free drink and it wasn't long before people were laughing and joking with us, asking us what we were doing in La Ceiba.

One sad thing about that evening was, when we spoke about the church down the road, which we were helping to build, one young man said he could never go there because they wouldn't accept people who drank beer. Now, that may have been completely wrong, but that was his reality and it's people's realities that we need to change.

People's perceptions of church and Christianity can be completely off the mark at times. I hope that young man's reality was changed a little that evening as Wes and I sat in his environment, laughing and joking with him... 'The Great Love' can see God's treasure everywhere.

Two things last forever – the Word of God, and people. God doesn't treasure anything more than He treasures people... Men and women, boys and girls, the young and the old, they are the treasure of His heart... If only we could truly understand that... then maybe we would leave our cosy church and go and live among those who are God's lost treasure.

Why? Why did Jesus spend more time with His friends in low places than He did with those who ran the religious establishment?

I believe it is because Jesus accepted them for who they were and they accepted Jesus for who He was. And that allowed the treasure in Jesus' life and the treasure in the low places to be unearthed.

Hidden treasure in you

It is much easier to see the potential in another person than in yourself. But the truth is, there is hidden treasure in all of us.

I remember when I was younger, my dreams were very real to me, and I couldn't see any reason why they would not come true. When you are younger, you take everything in your stride and still believe that you can do what you are dreaming of doing, while becoming who you are dreaming of becoming.

What happens to those unfulfilled dreams as we grow up? They get buried under the mundane disappointments and mistakes of our life. These, along with increasing responsibilities, bury our dreams.

Another shovel of dirt is piled on, and then another rock, until the treasure that we were born with, which is the real us, becomes forgotten and lost forever, unless it's unearthed.

It's like being in the belly of a whale.

Unearth our dreams... it sounds easy, but you and I both know it's not. Facing a lack of personal confidence and, often, self-belief, we struggle to pick ourselves up and reach higher... but the reality is, unless we start, our lives won't change and the treasure that is within us, placed there by God Himself, will never be seen and enjoyed by our world.

We need to be obedient to God's will and purpose for our lives, in every aspect.

I can't tell you how many battles I have had in my mind over writing this book. I started writing this chapter at a time when as a family we had lost everything we had... I will talk more about that later on. My confidence and self-belief had taken the biggest battering I'd ever had in my life, and my mind would tell me, 'No one will publish this book and if there is a person out there nutty enough to do so, then no one will buy it... It's going to be a big mistake and great disappointment to you, so just don't write it.'

My head is a real mess at times... just like yours... don't deny it!

With the love and encouragement of my wife, Sharron, and the friends that from time to time ask me, 'When are you writing that book?', I have decided to reach higher, unearth a dream and see where it takes me. If I believe God created me, then I will believe that He did so for a purpose, and it's that purpose which is the treasure I carry... I want to share that treasure with the world... not to be praised and glorified, but to show the miracle that if God can use a muppet like me, then He can use a muppet like you! ☺

You have treasure that this world needs... Dig deep and believe again that you can see your dreams come to pass. You may have to rearrange your life a little but whatever you do, don't let your past disappointments turn into fear, because that fear will keep you down unless you conquer it.

Don't let the belly of this world keep the treasure that you are hidden any longer!

LIVING

IN THE MARGINS

Chapter Two: Living in the Margins

I was in my local pub on a Saturday evening. I had just been to see Sheffield United play at Bramall Lane and was now hanging out with some fans and enjoying a beer. It was a lively, happy atmosphere where men were merry from the drink and the football win. The air was filled with friendly banter and some colourful language... As I took the experience in, I became aware that I was enjoying myself more than some do on a Sunday morning.

I love being in the places that you don't find any or few Christians in. I believe these places are desperate for God's great love and the light of the gospel. The problem is that these places, where the gospel is desperately needed, are usually the same places that the gospel is hardest to find.

Every group of people marginalises those around them through their rules, regulations and traditions. Clubs, politics, music, sports etc. all create margins in which those who can't or won't live by their laws/rules/values are forced to live.

The Ku Klux Klan marginalise those who are not white; motorcycle groups like the Hell's Angels, Satan's Slaves and Outlaws marginalise those who don't have a custom bike, like us Vespa riders. ☺

Football fans all over the world marginalise those who don't wear the same football shirt as themselves... you don't sit with the Sheffield United fans if you're wearing a Sheffield Wednesday shirt!

You may have had an experience where a church has pushed you into the margins because of their rules, regulations and traditions. I'm not taking about the BIG Ten (Ten Commandments); in fact, the BIG Ten should only inspire us to live a better life with God and with the world, but it is usually the way they are communicated that pushes people away, not the commandments themselves.

Margins of people outside of the mainstream Church are created because of their rules, regulations and traditions. Often these are manmade and are based upon the group's likes and dislikes, what they believe to be a right and wrong way to live and conduct yourself. And so we find ourselves preaching a message that is all-inclusive but excluding those who don't fit in with us. That is not the gospel or the life that Jesus modelled for us to live out.

Imagine with me for a moment two pieces of paper: one is lined and has a margin on the left side; the other is blank.

Blank pages are more fun...

...no lines to restrict you in the direction you want to draw or write in, and no margin that reduces the area in which you can create.

Lined pages are restrictive... You have to write on the lines that have already been set out for you; if you cross the lines it just looks messy and awkward. The margin is rarely used; you may place a number in there, or a letter at some point, but by and large it remains untouched and unused. Unless you fill it with corrections.

Now, imagine with me... about your life and the church or Christian community that you attend or lead. Which page represents them the best?

Is it a lined page?... Restricted, with a set of rules and guidelines on which you have to live out your life? And a margin that has many people in it who are not like you and can't live on the same lines as you do, which means that you never mix with them?

Or is it blank?.. No rules or restrictive guidelines which have been made by a man or a religious group; no likes and dislikes and no margin? A life in which all kinds of people with all kinds of hobbies, social activities and of all classes mix freely with respect and love? A life where the BIG Ten are our only boundaries?

I believe many churches talk about reaching those in the margins, but don't realise that these margins exist because the same churches have created lines by which you have to live if you are going to belong and be a part of them.

'You can't play football on a Sunday morning.'

'You shouldn't dress that way.'

'We don't drink alcohol.'

'You can't be fully committed unless you come to all the church services.'

'You need to let us know how much your tithes and offerings will be each week.'

'You're not prosperous enough.'

'You shouldn't socialise in those places.'

'You shouldn't listen to secular music.'

'If you go to college/university, it should be a Christian one.'

'We don't allow women to read publicly from the Bible.'

'Don't wear that jewellery.'

'Your kids are too disruptive... control them.'

'You're the wrong colour.'

'You need to jump around more during worship.'

'I wouldn't do or say that, if I were you; the pastor wouldn't like it.'

'You work where?!'

...and so on and so on.

It doesn't take long for men and women, young and old, to discover these lines that we draw, and when they do, they realise that they won't ever belong – I mean fully belong – unless they live on the lines... and when you don't belong, you don't stay around.

It's our religious rules, just like the Pharisees and Sadducees of Jesus' day, that create marginalised people. And it's these people, the ones who are marginalised, that Jesus came to seek and to save.

Living on lined paper

Many people live their lives on lined paper, as do many churches. Everything has to be structured and remain the same – living on lines that often have to be manmade to make life easy to handle, and safe. Lines... rules, dos and don'ts, can and cannot – boundaries that stop you wandering too far from what is now your custom and lifestyle. Restrictions that hold you in from exploring.

We as Christian communities/churches or as individual disciples can easily create lines (what we will and won't allow) and thus create margins filled with those who do what we won't allow or accept. The church that preaches against alcohol will create a line that their congregation must live on, and for those that can't or won't, they either hide it and pretend, which will result in the church not really getting the real man or woman, or they will be pushed into the margin and often left alone by the church.

Individuals, through their attitudes, create lines. You may not like or agree with tattoos, but does that line you draw stop you meeting and mixing with those who are tattooed or tattoo?

Lines that we create can be a number of things: e.g. standing against the use of alcohol and tobacco, tattoos and piercings, listening to secular music, clothing, the places you socialise, your job, the language you use, how often you should attend church services, betting, playing sports or attending a sporting event on a Sunday, buying a Sunday newspaper, going to see an 18 (R-rated) movie... the list can go on and on.

I remember my grandad (who was a church minister) wouldn't buy a Sunday newspaper as it condoned working on a Sunday. It wasn't until I got older that I figured out Sunday's papers were made on Saturday; it was Monday's paper that caused people to work on Sunday!

> **The gospel, 'Good News of Jesus', is for everyone; it's for the everyday people in the everyday places.**

But a problem occurs when those everyday places become the margins of life, because we or our Christian communities have created a regimented and restricted form of Christianity, which holds us in and back from those everyday places with those everyday people.

When was the last time you sat next to someone in church and asked him or her if they had sniffed a line of coke that morning? When was the last time you got together with your Christian friends and never let go of your handbag or jacket for fear that it may be stolen? Or when was the last time you went to court with a friend who was standing before the judge for assault? And here is one more... when was the last time you sat in a pub and talked about the struggle many middle-aged men have with depression and not realised that one of the men at the table had recently tried to kill himself?

People who live on lined paper don't have friends, conversations or moments like that because all those people have been forced to live in the margin that our religious lifestyle has created.

The reality is that unless we change, unless we begin to rub out some of those lines and break into the margins, allowing the marginalised to flow into our lives, we will never see everyday people touched by the greatest love of all... God Himself. And like you, I still believe for a great revival to sweep England, Europe and the world.

There will be some reading this that believe we (Christians) should be in the world and not of it... that we are called to come out and be separate from the world etc. There will be others who don't give a s*@! about those who have yet to meet 'The Great Love' and that is evident because their lives are consumed in a Christian bubble. They are Christian consumers who devour every service they can get to, always buying the latest book to come out (including this one) and socialise only with those who have a Christian fish on their car. My brief answer to this is: 'Take a look at Jesus.' Other than Jesus inviting His disciples to take some time out in a quiet place with Him or eat a meal with Him as He did with the Last Supper, I don't recall Jesus inviting people to church, His house or a church picnic... He was the one being invited or inviting Himself to where everyday people were.

We are called to be separated from sin, but not from the sinner. All the time modelling the BIG Ten... God's boundaries for life.

Living on plain paper

Jesus didn't create margins... He stood against the rules and regulations that the religious institution of His day had put in place. He didn't come to live on the lines and ignore those who didn't want to be a part of the establishment. He came to show us how to live a free life and at the same time love God with all our hearts, souls and strength, and then love our neighbours as we love ourselves.

Jesus' neighbours were just like ours today – male and female, young and old, drinkers and overeaters, sex mad and perverters of godly living. But He didn't hide from them... He lived on a blank page, He lived among them... Emmanuel, God with us!

Over the coming chapters I will be sharing my experiences of living in the margins, cultivating a life on a blank page which at times is very uncomfortable and painful, but at other times is beautiful and greatly rewarding.

If God is omnipresent (everywhere all the time), and I believe He is... then God right now is in the pub and bar down the street. He is with the homeless. He is sitting with the children who are caught up in the divorce-fuelling arguments in their home. He is with the depressed man who thinks his family are better off without him. He is with the college and university students who are abusing their first taste of real freedom with sexual acts and alcohol abuse. He is standing at the door of the brothels, travelling with Satan's Slaves, Hell's Angels and the Outlaws. He is with the football hooligans across Europe. He is in the abortion clinic. He is in the hospital waiting rooms, the unemployment lines, the poor housing estates, slums, townships and projects, the drug dens, nightclubs and porn industry...

God, 'The Great Love', is everywhere all the time

I wonder what He is doing in all those places with all those people?

I wonder what 'The Great Love' is trying to say and show?

I wonder if Christians (Christ-like people) should go and discover what God is doing in the margins?

Maybe 'The Great Love' is just waiting for us to get involved?

BREAKING
THE SILENCE

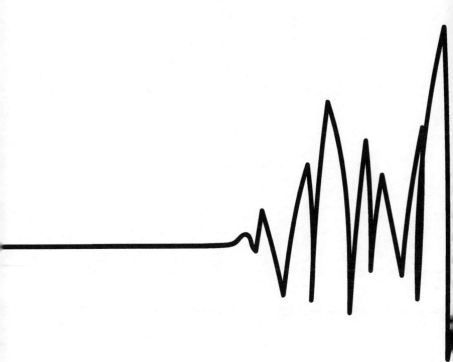

Chapter Three: Breaking the Silence

A changing world – a stubborn Church

I will never forget 1977 and the years leading into the 1980s.

I was living on a council estate minding my own business and doing what all kids do, playing football, riding my bike, spraying my name on the subway walls at the back of our house and enjoying a bag of chips from the chippy whenever I could. I was enjoying life and the innocence of it.

I don't know exactly where I was or what I was doing when I heard it, but the music that my young ears were to pick up would cause me to change.

Punk music had arrived.

I loved it!

There was something about the punk movement that gripped my heart and caught my attention like nothing else. I was excited by the drive of the music and the ferocious lyrics that challenged ideals and asked questions. Its discontent with the norm was shown through its style of clothes and haircuts. The boots, ripped jeans, spiked hair or Mohawk, my leather jacket with 'The Exploited' painted on the back, I loved that it didn't fit into mainstream thinking and fashion... There was an uprising taking place and I wanted to be a part of it.

> **The silence of my life had been broken**

I heard lyrics, beats and rhythms and would never be the same again. I experienced a loss of innocence, if you like, since I had been brought up in a Christian family, going to church every Sunday both in the morning and at night. But I didn't see the revolution there as I did in the punk scene.

Church didn't offer adventure. The dress code, the music, the way people communicated didn't excite me. Don't get me wrong, I look back on those years with great fondness and am truly thankful for the morals that I learned and the knowledge of the Bible that I gained – all of which has helped me to this day.

But, even at a young age, I wanted revolution. I wanted to be different. I needed to discover me through what was happening both within the Church and without. I wanted to live on a blank page, not on the lines.

The problem was that as the world was changing, the Church remained the same. It refused to become culturally relevant and more lines were drawn... you can't come to church in studs, with coloured hair and half a tube of wood glue keeping it standing up. And the music, you had no chance... back then most churches still only had an organ or piano; guitars and drums were the devil's instruments.

I remember as a kid going to church and watching old Mrs Cooper sat at the piano playing as loudly as she could. She insisted on wearing a hat and a big overcoat all year around. I know a few deacons wanted to try to soften the sound of the piano, so they stuffed cushions inside it... and when it was time to move the piano from its regular spot, they had to do so just a couple of inches a week, to not upset Mrs Cooper. I think everybody was breathing a sigh of relief when she finally put her hat and overcoat on for the last time and left for heaven.

How can instruments be of the devil? How can anything be the devil's creation? The devil can't create anything, he is not a creator, but what he is, is a perverter; he takes God's creation and perverts it... I believe punk music was and is God's creation, but there are streams of it that have been perverted and misused. That is one of the reasons why hell is going to be unbearable... it's going to be void of music, the music is all going to be in heaven, the blues, jazz, hip hop, punk, metal, thrash, Brit pop... it's all going to be there... God may have pity on the devil and let him have one style of music and if He does... I reckon it will be country and western! :-)

From the Two Tone culture with bands such as Madness, The Selecter and The Specials to the skinhead scene with the Business, the Blitz, 4-Skins and Sham 69 and the punk scene with the Sex Pistols, The Clash, Exploited and the Anti-Nowhere League, I explored, I became... I was living.

To this day the punk culture inspires me, the good and the bad of it. This, with my faith, has brought me to believe that Jesus Christ was a punk at heart. He broke the silence over 2,000 years ago!

Between the Old and the New

I have two blank pages in my Bible. Well, one of them is blank; the other has the words 'The New Testament' printed on it.

They are both together, side by side, one symbolising the end of the Old Testament and the other the beginning of the New Testament.

> **The end of the old and the beginning of the new, side by side**

These two pages represent a period in history of around 400 years, which is often referred to as the years of silence. It was during these years of silence that the Persians, the Greeks and then the Romans ruled the known world. It was during these 400 years that Alexander the Great lived.

God was active in the Old Testament speaking to people through dreams, burning bushes, visions and prophets. He spoke about things that were to come in the future. The book of Isaiah contains detailed descriptions of the Messiah, the one who was to come and save His people from their sins.

Years and years of prophecies followed with people talking about the day of redemption and the freedom from oppression that would come at the hand of the Son of God, the Christ, the Messiah.

Then all of a sudden… silence. Over 400 years of silence!

Silence does not always feel good, it does not always bring peace and calm with it. Silence is not always golden.

In Paul's letter to the Galatians, he writes: 'So also, when we were children, we were in slavery under the basic principles of the world. But when the time had fully come, God sent His Son, born of a woman, born under law, to redeem those under law, that we might receive the full rights of sons' (Galatians 4:3–5).

'When the time had fully come.' What do you think that phrase means? Is it that brokenness had reached the top of the cup? Or that humankind had committed every sin possible and now the time had come for change? Was it that the established religion was forcing humanity away from God rather than enabling them to find God?… Whatever is meant by that phrase, one thing is for sure – a definite and certain time came for God to make the ultimate sacrifice and send His Son, Jesus, to live among humankind on earth… the time had come for God to break His silence.

Jesus didn't arrive as some foreign missionaries do. He came at His most vulnerable, as a baby. He lived in the heart of the community, same housing, same clothes and food, and worked in the community. Some missionaries today are so aloof from their communities; the margins that they have chosen to take 'The Great Love' to. They turn up with the latest 4x4, laptop and mobile phone, wearing designer clothes and usually live in accommodation of a much higher standard than those they are reaching. Missionaries like this are not truly embraced into the community; they never get treated like a neighbour because they are seen as a benefactor. The margins won't be honest with you until you rely on them as much as they rely on you; that is being incarnational and that is what God did, He came to live among us… Jesus was incarnational.

John 1:14 says: 'The Word became flesh and blood, and moved into the neighbourhood' (*The Message*). He came and lived among everyday people in everyday places. In fact, although He was born in a stable in a place called Bethlehem, He grew up in Nazareth. Nazareth was a tough place to grow up in, not unlike the urban estates that are all over the UK. The reputation of Nazareth was not a good one. When Philip told Nathanael, 'We have found the one that Moses wrote about in the Law, and about whom the prophets also wrote — Jesus of Nazareth, the son of Joseph', Nathanael replied, 'Nazareth! Can anything good come from there?' (John 1:45–46).

There are millions of people in the world that believe God is silent... men and women who haven't heard God speak to them in their lifetime... As far as they are concerned, God is silent. But God has broken the silence, and for those of us that have heard His voice and received 'The Great Love', we are now called sons and daughters of God... friends of God.

Jesus said to His followers when He went back to see them after His resurrection: 'Peace be with you! As the Father has sent me, I am sending you' (John 20:21).

We have been sent like Jesus was, to be incarnational, live in the heart of our communities and break down anything that creates margins and forces people away from God.

Are you breaking the silence of those around you?

Interrupting

Jesus came into this world breaking the silence, interrupting the norm with a message that was to change lives. One of His best mates, John the Baptist, wore a jacket made from a camel with a leather belt and went around eating locusts.

I can imagine kids seeing this guy and going home, looking for an old leather belt, ruffling their hair up and asking their dads for a camel-hair jacket and some locusts. They wanted to be like John... he was different... he was the voice of a revolution.

And Jesus was that revolution!

Jesus interrupted Church and culture; He challenged the way in which things were done and why they were done. He was infectious to those who chose to follow Him. He broke their silence and they were never to be the same again. The revolution was gathering momentum and, like the punk scene, some stood on the side and just watched with judgement, while others jumped in and became the scene.

Silence of friends

Martin Luther King, Jr said, 'In the end, we will remember not the words of our enemies, but the silence of our friends.'

Why does the silence of our friends hurt us more than the words of our enemies?

Is it trust? Have we placed a trust in such friends that leads us to believe that they have our back, as we have theirs?

Is it love? Have we allowed ourselves to believe that the love our friends have for us is the same as the love we have for them?

Is it loyalty? Have we hoped that our friends would actually take a bullet for us as they said they would?

Is it time? Have we invested time in creating a history with our friends; memories of fun days, holidays, and standing with them through life-changing decisions? Have we taken time to create a bond that money and pretence can't buy and that can be clearly seen by shared pictures in frames or on Facebook?

> Taking a bullet for a friend means, if your friend was faced with a great failure you would take it for them...

...if they were faced with a life-threatening illness you would gladly exchange places; if your friend was a victim of injustice, you would stand up for them, no matter the personal cost.

When a friend that you trust, love, and have invested your life into and would gladly take a bullet for lets you down by keeping silent when you are in need of their words of true friendship most, it brings a wound that is both deep and painful.

Some of us don't have to wonder or try to imagine what Jesus felt like that night when all of His close friends – the ones He trusted, loved, received promises of loyalty from, the ones He had poured His life into – deserted Him.

Some ran away — nowhere to be seen — and some stayed closer, but kept their distance, far enough away to not be associated with Him.

It was not the words of His enemies that Jesus would remember, but the silence of His friends.

It's still the silence of His friends that wounds Him today. Those followers who have received Him and are called 'Christian' who keep the good news to themselves and don't break the silence as Jesus did. There are lives desperate to hear about and experience 'The Great Love' and because of the lines on our page, we refuse to take it to where it is desperately needed and hardest to find. Jesus looks on and weeps... the silence of His friends wounding Him again.

Not long after being abandoned and left to die, Jesus would come back and break the silence of His close friends as they gathered together in remorse and fear.

'Peace be with you! As the Father has sent me, I am sending you' (John 20:21).

That moment, in the showing of true forgiveness, He displayed the true meaning of trust, love and loyalty. He offered them many more days to create a history together.

He broke the silence by taking the bullet of punishment for them.

He gladly gave up the remainder of His life on earth so that they would be able to live the remainder of their days as free men.

Men living free... breaking the silence and taking 'The Great Love' into the margins.

Turning up the volume

Every parent has said it because every teenager has done it!

'Turn that down!' is what gets shouted in the direction of the teenager's bedroom.

I loved listening to music in my bedroom when I was younger. This was back in the day when the only options you had were either vinyl seven-inch singles and twelve-inch LPs or a cassette tape. There were no MP3s, CDs or satellite radio. I'm feeling old just writing this.

My bedroom was my castle... it was my world... my place to shut the world out and dream of what I would do with my life in the coming years. I would lay down on my bed with one of my records playing, with the volume way up high... absorbed into the sounds, transported to a future world where I was gifted, talented and free, a world in which I brought joy to people, a world where I was loved and happy.

My space (I'm not talking about the internet but the original *my space*... my bedroom) would be filled with the sounds of my choosing; not giving a second thought as to how far my music would travel beyond my kingdom, I would lay back and enjoy the environment I had created.

And then it comes, the booming voice from downstairs: 'Turn that music down!'

Reality has invaded your kingdom and you're back to living life with the volume set at normal.

I believe more of us need to turn up the volume of our lives and let the song that God has given us play out across our world. I remember as a young man something significantly changing in me. I can only describe it as an explosion of love within.

I was in church one Sunday morning at the age of eighteen. I was thankful to be in a growing church, one that everyday people could come to, but it still had its traditions – lines drawn that stopped some in the margins coming. I won't tell you what happened when I got my ear pierced in that church or when I went to the movies three times in one weekend, I'll leave that for another book... Back to the story... I was stood in the morning service during the praise and worship and I can only explain what happened as a beautiful awakening to the needs of others around me, which was accompanied by a burning desire to live in such a way that the needs of others would be met by my actions of love. 'The Great

Love' had exploded within me...

The transformation of my life that was to take place from that moment on was to do so from within, not without.

When you are told to live a certain way – the Bible calls it 'Living by the Law' – you obey rules and regulations and the change comes to your life from the outside. But when you are filled with God 'The Great Love' and His Holy Spirit lives within you, the changes come from within and not by living on the lines; this is true spiritual transformation, and it's not just a moment. This transformation is in process for the rest of your life here on earth. That's why it's so important to stay friends with God; it's through friendship with Him that you become the man/woman that you were created to be.

There is something so beautiful when you see a person grow in love. When the hardest of hearts begins to soften, when a person changes and becomes concerned about those around them, not just themselves, there is an awakening of true love, not selfish love but sacrificial love. The volume of their life gets turned up.

When Jesus arrived on this earth, God was turning up the volume.

God's love exploded in history through the presence and actions of His Son, Jesus.

As Jesus developed through His childhood, adolescence and into manhood, the desire to act upon the love that was burning within Him began to grow. He was now living in a different room to that which He was used to, a different castle and a different world.

He had come from heaven and brought with Him the unforgettable melodies of that kingdom. His actions of love were like tunes that would never be forgotten.

He kept putting His hand on the sound control and steadily turning up the volume. He turned water into wine and up went the volume level. He spent time with the social outcasts and up went the volume. He stood in the graveyard and raised a man from the dead and up went the volume. He loved all those who came to Him unconditionally, from the ones who did life well to the ones who struggled... and up went the volume.

And then, one weekend the time came in which the volume was turned up all the way. The religious shouted out at the top of their voices, 'Turn the volume down!'... so after He took the beating of a lifetime, they hung Jesus on a cross, and the volume was turned up to the last notch... the music was deafening, but still the voices of the religious fathers shouted, 'Turn it down!'

Jesus breathed His last... The religious, with their lined paper of dos and don'ts, finally thought they had shut the rebellious God fanatic up... But you can't just bury truth; truth will always rise to the surface. You can't just shut 'The Great Love' away because the yearning and calling out for love from the human heart will cause 'The Great Love' to find its way to them.

While Jesus was put out of sight in a tomb, He walked into hell for the keys of life and death and all of hell heard the beautiful victorious melody of His life as He took hold of the keys. His triumphant song would not just stop there; three days later He would bring it back to the earth, and forty days later in an upper room He would give it to 120 everyday people, who would take His song at high volume and travel across the world.

When the song found a home in the hearts of those who listened, the volume of Christianity, the volume of Love, and the volume of God's message were turned up. 'The Great Love' was breaking the silence of everyday lives in everyday places.

Not once during Jesus' sacrificial life did His heavenly Father shout out from heaven, 'Turn that noise down.' He was well pleased with His Son's actions, for they were like an infectious song that brings peace, joy, hope and courage, the type you can't stop listening to or humming.

In fact, God was dancing to the music of love and revolution the louder it got.

Is your heavenly Father enjoying the music of your life as the volume gets turned up by your actions of love? Or is He shouting out, 'Turn that noise down!'?

Are you willing to break the silence?

BREAK
OUT

Chapter Four: Breakout

'Break Out' — Foo Fighters

I don't do well sat at a desk or in business meetings. I have a very short attention span, unless I am watching football. My mind wanders and I daydream about committing acts of outrageous courage and significance.

Committee meetings just do my head in... sat around discussing the colour a wall should be painted, how short the grass should be cut; should we have nice soft toilet roll or that sharp, shiny stuff that has no grip, because it's cheaper? These kind of meetings just wind me up, especially when it gets round to discussing the important issues of reaching our communities with the gospel. At that point my sanity is pushed to the limit because you always find someone who says it will cost too much, take too long, upset too many people, bring too much change or make some feel uncomfortable. I think for some church committees it is very fitting that they are called by the same name as a group of vultures... a group of vultures is called a committee.

I function best in a team where I am able to leave the committee stuff to those who enjoy it and have a gift for the mundane detail, but at the same time a passion to get the gospel and 'The Great Love' out into the everyday places.

Wars are won with two things – treasure and blood. Nations supply the finance to purchase weapons, planes, battleships, tanks etc. and people supply the blood... the soldiers and their families. I am more of a solider than a war-room treasurer.

In the year 2000 my family and I moved to the city of Sheffield in South Yorkshire. Sheffield is a beautiful city; it currently has two championship football teams, two universities and is on the doorstep of the Peak District, a beautiful national park. With nearly three-quarters of a million people making it the fourth largest city in England, it gives you some things you don't normally see in village or small-town life, like the punk lady who walks her ferret on a lead around the alternative part of the city, or the naked man who rides his bicycle in the summer; well... he looks naked from a distance but closer up you can see that he is wearing a very small, shiny blue G-string... I feel sick! I remember seeing him one day riding towards me and as he got close I shouted,

> **'Oi! Put some clothes on!'**

...at which he shouted back, 'Oi! Take some clothes off!' – a perfect example of two men physically in the same place but living in two very different realities.

On arriving in Sheffield I came out of working for a youth missions' organisation. I had found Christians surrounded my life in my workplace and in my social life. Moving to Sheffield gave me an opportunity to serve a good friend of mine, Phil Cana, in the church he is leading, but also work back in the secular world and to find myself some non-church friends.

I started working for the City Council in their youth service department. I was doing detached and youth club work in the roughest parts of Sheffield...

> **I wanted to get back into the margins,**
> **and boy, did I get a wake-up call...**

...working with the youth in those areas. Some of these girls saw giving a blow job to a lad as no different to stealing a can of coke... teenagers ready to rob and fight at any opportunity, living day to day, staying out till the early hours and then not going to school... teenagers who weren't loved very well.

I have fond memories of those years, being attacked with a pool cue, taking some of them out for a trip and realising when we got back to the minibus they had been shoplifting in all the places we had been. If any place or any group of people needs 'The Great Love' in their lives, it is the kids and teenagers growing up in the poorest parts of our nations, on the urban estates.

Shortly after arriving in Sheffield, I picked up a book on its nightlife... I was looking for somewhere to hang out and make some friends. Flicking through the book I came across a nightclub called 'The Corporation'... Just reading the short description of this club made me want to go. It was an alternative club for punks, skins, skaters, Goths, hardcore fans etc.; it even had a half-pipe inside the club itself.

I had a burning desire to break out of the Christian bubble I had found myself in. I had lost touch with the world around me. If you're a senior minister reading this, then let me encourage you to find someone in your congregation and go to one of your local nightclubs... stay out till 3am, go home smelling of beer and cigarettes (not because you have been drinking or smoking but because those around you have); there is a world of difference to hearing what goes on late at night in your town and city and experiencing it for yourself. I guarantee you one thing: if 'The Great Love' is in you, then you will be moved when you see those in that environment. They stop being distant figures and become people with real personalities and stories. Your preferences are pushed to the back of the line and love comes ferociously to the front, and if you love well... they become friends.

Read the signs

I remember one day just sitting quietly and thinking about my life and future. I wasn't happy with who I had become, and my Christian walk had become dull. I felt like I was locked in a cell, isolated from the world, and that troubled me. I had become so self-righteous and inward-looking, but how could I break out? How could I really live life again in such a way that was authentic and godly? I knew something had to change, and that something was actually someone... me. I needed God to guide me, to give me a sign, point me in the right direction.

I wrestled with how disconnected I had become with those that I would pass on the street, see in the supermarket and sit with in restaurants. The dark places that I would encourage people to stay away from were now calling to me; I was desiring to go into them to spend time with those who went there.

How could I? How could I come out of this imitation world I was breathing in and walk the streets that everyday people were walking? How could I be with them in spirit and not just body?

As I bowed my head, I saw a tattoo on my arm that I have had for a number of years; it simply says 'Disciple'. A disciple is a follower, a pupil or student, one who is learning from and is devoted to the one they follow.

I have chosen to follow Jesus, His teachings and His example. I am His student and now He was going to teach me something I would never forget.

Go!

This one simple word came bursting through my mind, filling my imagination. I had not been asked or commanded to stay, but I had found myself living with an attitude that people should come to us and listen to what we had to say... 'Stay where you are and wait for people to come to you.' How arrogant and stupid that now sounds.

I was asked and commanded to GO! Go into the world, the streets, the dark places and bring out the flavour of life with the salt of the gospel.

I should be moving freely through the main streets, the side streets, the back streets, the homes of new friends, and the social occasions of those who still hadn't found what they were looking for. Compelling them to meet Jesus.

What was I waiting for?

I started counting the cost of the breakout. What would people say? 'He has a demon'? 'He spends too much time with unsavoury characters in unsavoury places'? 'He has backslidden and lost his faith'?

If I was to live, I mean really live, then I had to embrace the adventure that was offered to me. And that is what I did, when I picked up that book advertising all the dark places where the social occasions took place. I found one place that resonated within in me, so I set my goal and my sight on going.

There was no going back; only forward, no more waiting. The momentum forward had started by my decision to be a true disciple and 'GO'.

Friday nights would never be the same once I started hanging out at the 'Corp'... and I would never be the same. I was breaking out into the margins.

I was breaking out!

I'm shining the light on the darkest places

You know and I know we have to face this now

We have to face this now

I'm shining the light on the darkest places

Putting the word out we have to face this now

We have to face this now

'The Darkest Places' by MxPx from their album *Panic*.[1]

Friend of sinners

I will promise you one thing... When you start to break out of your Christian environment and head towards the margins, you will get those around you who will doubt your heart and will try to hold you back. You may not be at as many church functions or services as before and that can be seen as a walking away from God rather than a walking towards Him.

For John came neither eating nor drinking, and they say, 'He has a demon.' The Son of Man came eating and drinking, and they say, 'Here is a glutton and a drunkard, a friend of tax collectors and "sinners".' But wisdom is proved right by her actions. (Matthew 11:18–19)

When the religious leaders in Jesus' day called Him a 'friend of sinners', it was because they wanted to wound Him and discredit Him.

I believe Jesus showed great wisdom when He embraced this title that was given to discredit Him. He turned it around and embraced the words that were spoken with disdain and counted them as a compliment.

One thing this passage shows us is how religious people will never be happy when the true message of the gospel is preached. And that true message is that whoever comes to Christ will receive the greatest gift of all – they will become friends of God.

Before Jesus started His ministry, John the Baptist prepared the way for Him. John brought the message of confession and repentance to avoid the anger of God. He came neither eating regular food nor drinking, yet that did not satisfy the Jews.

John was not your normal sort of guy, he was a man who abstained, had a reclusive nature and a simple lifestyle. He did not seek out social occasions, choosing to live his own way, and the religious leaders assumed he had a demon or was just a complete nutcase.

After John came Jesus. Now, He did come drinking (that means alcohol) and eating; He had the same diet and appetite as any man. He joined in social occasions and was often invited to parties and people's homes. But even that didn't satisfy the religious Jews. They said He was a glutton and a drunk... a friend of sinners.

The point is not whether religion does or doesn't like drinking and parties etc. What the religious will always rise against is anything and anyone that threatens their way of life, their customs and convictions. That's why the Jews weren't happy with John or Jesus; it was their message that challenged their customs and convictions

– that's why they got ugly.

So how does the religious establishment respond? By speaking out against the messenger, often by personal attacks and then ignoring the message and carrying on as before.

As I have already mentioned, I was ready to break out from being a consumer of Christianity because when you live in a bubble like that, it is very easy to become unattached from the real world and arrested by a religious one. You begin to believe that unless people live the way you do, they won't be able to love God and receive God the way you do... How self-righteous and 'up myself' I had become.

I had to break out and into the margins; I had to spend time learning about those around me and being in their homes and at their parties (their places of entertainment). Their lives became of great importance to me. My love for those pushed away from the body of Christ had grown so much within me that 'The Great Love' compelled me to go.

This is when the adventure began; little did I know then how God would guide me through the dark places and cause me to shine with His grace and love.

Into the unknown

Jesus truly does inspire me... His life is an amazing read. Did you know the most shoplifted book in history is the Bible? This book has been nicked more than any other. I hope this generation won't let that statistic fall... Come on, let's keep the tradition alive, go and nick a Bible today from one of the local shops... let it be said of this generation, we played our part! (You know I'm joking, right?)

Jesus is one of these guys who says He loves you and then backs it up. He spent time with people in places they were comfortable with. I don't suppose He felt comfortable all the time but He pushed Himself because the lives of those who couldn't get to God through Church (the local synagogue) and the religious establishment were of immense importance to Him. He was drawn to them like a river is drawn to the sea, travelling the terrain, the twists and turns, unstoppable, determined to reach its destination.

I won't forget the first Friday night as I stood in line outside 'The Corporation' nightclub

Now, the 'Corp' didn't open till 10pm so I had to adjust to late nights and getting home in the early hours on a Saturday morning. As I stood there with a good friend of mine who was a youth evangelist for a local church, I felt nervous. I had been out of this scene for so long, I felt like I was visiting another planet. One thing I was looking forward to was the half-pipe skate ramp that was inside. Skating and alcohol don't mix, so if nothing else I was going to see some very funny skate moves.

All around us were young men and women who expressed themselves in creative ways through their hair, clothes, piercings and tattoos. There were those who had no hair, hair just down the middle, short hair, long hair and every colour hair you could imagine. Every kind of piercing was on show, including some very impressive ear stretching.

As the doors opened and we entered the club, we paid our entrance money and made our way inside. It was a big place and we spent time walking around and getting familiar with our new environment. It was dark, smelled of stale cigarettes and beer, and for some reason I felt at home; that was worrying and, at the same time, exciting.

I didn't have to be there long before my attention was firmly fixed on those who were around me. I wondered what the story of their lives was. What did they do during the day? What was their home-life like? What dreams did they have for the future?

In the UK you only have to be eighteen to gain entrance into a nightclub and drink alcohol (in America it's twenty-one). But whatever the benchmark is for the age of consent, there is always a large element of underage drinkers and clubbers. And it was that that first shocked me; I couldn't believe how many kids were in there from their mid-teens, smoking, drinking and fooling around. Then it was the content of some of the music that my attention was drawn to, for example 'Last Resort' by Papa Roach and 'My Generation' by Limp Bizkit.

If you read the lyrics online, I ask you with compassion, please don't get offended. This is the reality lots of people live with. If we get offended by learning about their cultures and lifestyles, that offence will stop us from loving them on their doorstep, they will miss out on 'The Great Love' and that is one thing every Christian should never let happen.

Something happened in me that night, something holy... I had broken out of the Christian bubble and my love for God had collided with a renewed love for people. There was no going back, I didn't want to go back; I wanted somehow, some way, to introduce these young men and women to 'The Great Love'.

My wife tells me I have an overactive imagination, and I think she is right, but on that night I started to imagine what the 'Corp' would look like if the kingdom of God came into it.

I grew up saying the Lord's Prayer, and the words 'your kingdom come, your will be done on earth as it is in heaven' (Matthew 6:10) had always stuck with me. I even have the words 'Your Kingdom Come' tattooed on my forearm. I began to understand that Jesus took the kingdom of God with Him wherever He went.

Once, having been asked by the Pharisees when the kingdom of God would come, Jesus replied, 'The kingdom of God does not come with your careful observation, nor will people say, "Here it is," or "There it is," because the kingdom of God is within you' (Luke 17:20–21).

We are carriers of God's kingdom... wherever we go, God's kingdom goes. Just think about all those prayers kids have prayed in school when they have said the Lord's Prayer or when in church the congregation say it together out loud. When we pray 'your kingdom come' we are asking God to transform us from within by His Holy Spirit and then we are to allow Him to guide us into places and people's lives where our actions become the evidence that His kingdom has come on earth and His will is being done on earth as it is in heaven.

So if I carry God's kingdom within me and at the same time God is omnipresent, everywhere all the time, then walking into the margins was for me discovering what God was already doing there and with compassion and wisdom, getting involved, working hand in hand with God.

When you enter the margins it won't be long before you start rubbing the lines out on your paper... lives become more important than the dos and don'ts.

New friends

You never know when a new friend is going to enter your life.

It can be a day like any other when you meet someone new and there is a connection between you both. The connection can come because you laughed over the same story, like the same music, have similar backgrounds, enjoy the same places of entertainment, or because one of you reached out with love when the other was in need of some care.

As I returned each Friday night to the 'Corp', my face became more familiar. It wasn't long before people would start nodding or raising their chin at me (their way of saying 'hi') and random conversations would take place.

One of those conversations was with Punk Joe.

Joe was a tall punk with a bright red Mohawk and more attitude than a steaming hot curry. He got his name 'Punk Joe' from never turning down a fight and always sticking up for his friends and those who were being picked on by someone bigger than themselves. The cuts and scars on his fists from fighting were his medals of honour.

The first time Joe and I spoke, we were sat in the little café inside the 'Corp' having a chip butty together. We talked about music, which was a real education for me. I had been out of this scene for so long that I didn't know all the new bands, and if I didn't know the bands and their music, then I wouldn't know what my new friends believed.

After talking about music, drugs and good times, Joe asked me what I did for a job. Now, I always get nervous when I am asked that question, because when I say I am a minister, pastor, vicar or preacher, I get one of two responses, one being 'goodbye' and the other, 'You got to be f*^\$@!* joking.'

On this occasion I got neither of those responses, I just got a tough punk called Joe look at me and with gentleness say, 'I've had some connection with Church through my family.'

That night a new friendship started between 'Andy the vicar' (that was the name I would be given) and 'Punk Joe'. Joe was a young man who couldn't do anything half-heartedly; if he was in, then he was in with everything. That's what made him a leader in the 'Corp' scene: others would look up to him, watch how much he could drink, how many joints he could smoke and what number of pills he could pop in a night. It amazes me how he is still alive, but he is, and I will tell you a bit more about Joe in a few minutes.

After I met Joe, he introduced me to a lot of new people. Joe was very popular and his friends became mine.

It wasn't long before I would start meeting up with my new friends at times other than Friday night. I had entered the world of these young men and women and had become a part of it, not just a visitor.

Jesus received His title 'friend of sinners' while hanging out with ordinary people in ordinary places and gaining friends by reaching out with love. I received my title 'Andy the vicar' by doing the same.

Over the years I've heard what has happened to some of those young men and women. Sally was a young woman with an infectious personality, and was a great people person; that's probably why she was so good at dealing drugs. But it was her father who found her dead in her flat from an overdose. Then there was Billy who couldn't kick the habit of drugs and was found dead in his bedroom, at the age of twenty-one, by his mum. Young lives tragically stolen and families brutally wounded by the dark side of life. Others have moved on and got an education and others are still trapped in a life of mundane jobs, social drug-taking and weekends of casual sex and drinking.

Joe is now in his early thirties and looks like an old-school skinhead, with his six foot-plus stature, shaved head, Fred Perry braces and boots; you can't miss him when he walks into a room.

Joe has recently unclenched his fists and raised his hands in surrender to 'The Great Love' and the change in this man is evident. It is the God who is on the inside of him that brings the changes, not the rules set around him. I can't tell you how much joy I felt recently as I stood with Joe in a tank of water on his baptism. To hear him confess his faith in God and desire to be a follower of the way made me realise that the seeds you sow may take ten years to grow... but they do grow.

I still see others from those days in the 'Corp'. Dan is a young man who a number of years ago tried to kill himself with an overdose. He had left home at sixteen and was living with a bunch of kids in a flat. When they found him they called me first and I met them all outside the hospital. Driving to the hospital at around 11pm I felt a great sadness over Dan. I have a son and I just couldn't imagine him going through life the way Dan was, and it wasn't all his choice; what does a young man do when the safe place of home becomes a war zone and a place of deep wounds? He runs and looks for love in all the wrong places, and our Father in heaven watches with tears in His eyes, hoping that in those places there will be a man or woman who is carrying His kingdom, waiting to love them well.

I still see Dan in my local; we talk from time to time. He is still searching and I am still loving him. He thanks me for all that I did for him in his younger years and we enjoy our friendship. I hope he finds 'The Great Love' that his heart and soul is longing for, and until that day my role in his life is to be his friend and love him in such a way that the kingdom of God can be clearly seen.

A small prayer answered

Often in life you get faced with the decision that if something is worth doing, are you going to do it alone if you have to?

One Friday night when preparing to go to the 'Corp', my mate phoned me and said he couldn't make it. I was faced with a decision: should I stay or should I go? (That's a Clash song!)

No one likes to go out alone. I remember a time when I was travelling in America and I got stuck in Orlando, Florida for a weekend on my own, which is no fun at all. I decided to go to Universal Studios and left after only experiencing two rides. I couldn't take the ride attendants asking me, 'How many in your party, sir?' I would answer by placing my finger and thumb in the shape of an L on my forehead and saying, 'Just the one.'

I find no fun in doing fun stuff alone.

But on this particular night I decided to go it alone to the 'Corp'. When I arrived the line was a long one to get in. Groups of people laughing, smoking, sharing stories together, all looking forward to a fun night out. I was there to have fun, but that was not the first thing on my list; I was there to make friends and shine.

I remember that night really well: it was a cold one and the feelings of being on my own were running high in me. As I stood in line I started to pray. It was a simple prayer: 'Father, would You bring me someone to hang out with tonight?'

I had no sooner finished praying than a young man walked up to me and said, 'Are you here on your own tonight?' I said, 'Yeah.' With a smile on his face he reached out his hand to shake mine and said, 'My name is Ray and I work in the "Corp". Each night I work I can get a friend in for free. You wanna come in with me?'

'Mate,' I replied. 'That would be great.'

I followed Ray to the door, which was firmly guarded by two of the biggest and meanest-looking bouncers. Ray just said to them, 'He's with me' and with a nod of the head they both stood aside and opened the door to let us in.

I wondered at that point what Ray's job was, so I asked. I was not prepared for the reply that I got: 'I work in the gents' toilets. I sit in there all night to make sure they don't get smashed up. We've had a couple of nights recently where guys have gone in fighting and smashed up the basins and that.'

I immediately had an idea; if Ray worked in the gents' toilets, he would know a lot of people. Everyone has to take a leak at some point in the night... I reckoned Ray could put names to the faces that I saw each Friday, so I asked him if I could hang out with him that night and he said yes.

I don't know what your experiences of toilets are, but mine are quite varied. I've had the privilege of travelling a lot and the toilets from country to country vary. I went to some public toilets once in Romania, and as you went in you paid the lady for two sheets of toilet paper that resembled woodchip wallpaper, and then when you had used them, you placed them in a basket at the door on the way out... I know, I know, but when in Rome...

I stayed in a house in Poland once that had its bathroom and kitchen in the basement and it was all open plan... no joke... You could have a bath while watching Mum cook the tea. I waited till late in the night to go down to the toilet, hoping to get the place to myself. As I sat there all I could think about was what I was going to do if someone walked in... so I decided to sing to let people know that I was on the toilet. The random thing is, the only song I could think of was a hymn that Sharron and I had at our wedding: 'What a Friend We Have in Jesus'... until that time I never knew how hard it was to go to the toilet and sing at the same time. Try it, it's not as easy as it sounds.

Then there was a time when I was travelling with my good friends Phil Cana and Chris Perry in America. We were sat in the airport in Detroit waiting for a forty-minute flight to Kalamazoo. We were chatting and drinking and completely lost track of the time until we heard our names called out over the speaker system: 'Would passengers Cana, Perry and Rushworth please make their way to gate number twenty-six...' We grabbed our bags and ran to the plane. As we were running I'm needing a number one but thought I could wait to go on the plane. When getting on to the plane I realised that this was not a flight in great demand, as the plane only held twenty people, and guess what... there was no toilet on it!

All I can say is that there is a point when a man can't hold it any longer and at that point you are white, sweating and feeling real sick and dizzy. Fortunately, the guy sat across the aisle to me fell asleep real quick, so I reached for the sick bag, shuffled on to the edge of my seat and filled that sick bag up. I don't know what I must have looked like walking off that plane with a bag full of pee.

Anyway.... the toilets in the 'Corp' were not great. Usually a couple of hours into the night the floor would be swimming with urine and the toilets would have various amounts of sick over them... It wasn't the best place to hang out, but to my amazement the guys would gather in there and chat about almost everything.

That Friday night I spent the whole time in the gents' toilets, with regular breaks to the bar to get my new friend Ray and me a drink. Ray introduced me to so many people that night, it was unbelievable. The faces that I had seen on a regular basis now had names to them, and they now knew my name: 'Andy the vicar'.

I know the gents' toilets sounds like a strange place to hang out and make friends, and by the end of the night the place stunk of pee and vomit — but maybe that is how Jesus' first night began in that stable in Bethlehem?

In my journey to 'break out' I had allowed God to guide me to the people and the places that needed His love, but I had lost the self-righteous attitude and became more concerned about the people than preaching a message. Even now as I type this I am washed with waves of emotion about this time in my life, about the people I met, the friends I made.

The cool thing about meeting Ray was that he went home and told his dad about me. His dad was a Christian who had been praying for his son for years. A week or so later, Ray's dad contacted me to thank me for being in the margins and to let me know he was praying for me.

> **You never know people's history**
> **until you get to know them...**

...and there is always that sad fact about many Christians that they are more concerned with preaching at people rather than getting to know them. I remember when I picked Ray up one Sunday morning and took him to church with me... he actually loved the worship and had his hands in the air, but the reality was, he just looked and sounded too different to fit in... the lines were too many to live up to and the margin looked like more fun anyway.

Everywhere I looked I could see buried treasure... treasure buried under the junk of life... treasure waiting to be discovered... treasure waiting to be restored.

WHEN THE
BOMBS FALL

Chapter Five: When the Bombs Fall

'If the Bombs Fall' (Larry Norman)

There will be a number of times when life doesn't go to plan and something hits you like a steam train right out of nowhere. I'm not talking about sitting next to a lady on a bus and asking her when the baby is due, at which point she looks at you and says, 'I'm not pregnant'... (true story); what I am talking about are those life-changing moments that happen through the storms of life.

The wisdom of Steve

I was sat in my local a few years ago with a good mate of mine, Steve.

Now Steve has a great testimony. Having not had the best of starts in life, Steve grew up tough and learned how to be a man on the street. Having been a professional doorman, he now trains young men in kick-boxing and cage fighting and runs successful tattoo parlours in Sheffield and Doncaster.

Steve will tell you that he became a Christian a few years ago now and the change in his life has been a good one. His initial year of surrendering his life to Jesus was a real transformation and the church he was a part of helped him greatly. But it wasn't long before Steve started to long for the honesty that he found in the pub to be in church.

While Steve and I were chatting about mainstream Church and the struggle for the men we know in the margins to connect with it, Steve came out with some great wisdom, which I have passed on many times since that night.

> 'Everyone has something to hide,' he said, 'but the one place we shouldn't have to hide anything is the one place we bury it the deepest... church.'

I believe that to be true. All of us crave honesty and a place where we don't have to hide who we really are. Church should be like that, a place where a person can be themselves and still be loved and valued. Not pretending to try to look better, which unfortunately many leaders do. You never seem to get the real them because they fear being transparent will cause their congregations to look at them as ordinary... well, guess what? They are ordinary; ordinary people whom God has chosen for a particular role in life and the Church. No matter how many books they write, sermons they preach and how big their church grows, they are still ordinary people changed by the love of God. And those in the margins need to see and hear that; it brings hope to the everyday people in the everyday places.

You want honesty?

We need more honesty in life, not so we can wallow in self-pity, but so that we can know we are not alone in our struggles. This in itself can bring hope: hope that our lives won't always be this way.

We need to be honest about life and not pretend that everything is great when we are actually hurting inside. In my experience, when life is difficult and has dealt you many wounds, it's through those wounds that God develops you and helps you understand what others are going through... it's through our struggles that we learn how to identify with others... that's why honesty is so important. I want to be able to identify with those in the margins... that is why I am going to be honest about an experience in my life that has dealt wounds deeper than I can express, and how God has used those events and memories to make my heart tender and aware of what is happening in the lives of those around me.

In Desmond Tutu's book *God Has a Dream*[2] he uses the illustration that suffering either transfigures you or embitters you. Suffering is a part of life; I wish it wasn't, but it is. How we deal with suffering will either transfigure us, in other words turn us into a more beautiful person, or embitter us, causing our lives to leave a bad taste and smell wherever we go.

We have the choice to go either way. I am thankful that it is because of my faith and belief in God and the Church that the suffering I am about to share with you has transfigured me and my family... Honour to God and the work of the Holy Spirit.

Thursday, 31 October 2002

Halloween... kids dressed up in scary costumes knocking on the door and asking, 'Trick or treat?' At that point, you're meant to give them some sweets (or candy, as our colonial friends say). But I have devised a new plan... Halloween is meant to be scary, right? Witches, vampires, foggy nights, ghosts and the Grim Reaper – so on Halloween I try to scare the kids that are trying to scare me. It's cruel, I know... but loads of fun! When I hear the knock on the front door, I creep up to the door so the kids can't hear me coming, I gently reach for the handle, take a deep breath and swing the door open really fast and at the same time let out a loud, horrifying scream which usually has the kids in complete panic. I even had the Grim Reaper in tears one year!

But Halloween has a very different meaning now for our family.

In the September leading up to Halloween in 2002, our middle child, Beth, had her seventh birthday. She was a pretty little girl with long blonde hair, all excited about having her birthday party at the Megacentre in Sheffield, where there is an amazing indoor play area.

A couple of days after her party, we noticed she was limping a little and there was a red patch in the back of her left knee. Over the next couple of days it got worse so we headed off to the children's hospital in Sheffield. The doctor believed it to be a muscle strain and sent us home.

The next couple of weeks saw Beth get worse, and she was now unable to stand. Back at the children's hospital the doctor thought it was now a bone infection, so Beth was admitted and hooked up to antibiotics. A week later we had our little princess home, who could now stand and walk as normal. But within a few days, a red patch appeared on her ankle and she started to complain of pain again.

This time when we arrived at the children's hospital, Beth was admitted, and over the next couple of weeks they did various tests to find out what was causing the pain our little girl was going through.

It was on Thursday, 31 October 2002 when they did the final test that was to be a lumbar puncture; this is where the doctor takes a sample of bone marrow out of the spine and examines it. At 4pm that afternoon Sharron and I were asked to go into a side room to talk with the doctor. The words that came out of his mouth hit us like a train coming out of nowhere: he told us our daughter had cancer in the form of leukaemia.

It's hard to explain the shock...

> **...I just sat there as Sharron began to cry.**

Sharron is a nurse, so she knew a lot about what was coming next, but all I knew was that cancer was treated by chemotherapy and you lost your hair. I can remember feeling numb; I guess that was the shock. I just kept thinking that things like this don't happen to families like ours.

Over the next hour the consultant talked us through what the next three years would be like in regards to treatment: how the coming twelve months would be filled with regular periods of intensive chemo, and what the effects of each period would look like and feel like for Beth. Chemo was going to start that evening and we would be moved to the cancer ward where more tests would be done which would enable the medical staff to know what type of leukaemia Beth actually had.

The good news at the beginning was that Beth had 'A.L.L.' leukaemia, which was the most common. Back then it held a success rate of just over 70 per cent based upon a girl of Beth's age. The other encouragement right at the beginning of treatment was that the cancer had been discovered relatively early. The leukaemic cells are created in the bone marrow; once that is full the cells then spill out into the bloodstream. That's why earlier blood tests that Beth had did not show that she had cancer: because the cells hadn't yet spilled out from the bone marrow.

I remember Sharron and I speaking with Beth, letting her know what was happening. It was difficult to remain composed while speaking with her, as the shock was still working through us, but we reassured her that she was going to get better... and thanks to God she is now twenty-one and training to be a children's nurse.

The events that unfolded over the next three years were many, but I want to share some of them with you. Some may surprise you, others may make you feel happy and compassionate, but what I do hope is that they deliver a level of honesty that will encourage you.

Sitting in silence

When Beth was diagnosed with leukaemia, I was working as a youth minister for a large Anglican church in the city of Sheffield. How we ended up in an Anglican church is another story. I actually have my ministerial credentials with the largest Pentecostal denomination in the world, so ministering in an Anglican church was a real experience and one that I would not change for the world.

The vicar back then was Peter Williams... even now as I write his name I am filled with much love for Peter and his wonderful wife, Mary. Peter was in his early sixties when I started working with him; he reminded me of my grandad, who passed away years earlier. With his pastoral qualities and a mind that was both made for theological matters and the ability to express them in a modern society, Peter's ability to bring change – and the change that was needed – was evident to all who had the privilege to share those years of ministry with him.

A sign of a great leader is when they let those they lead be themselves, and understand that at times they need to express themselves, which may not necessarily be done in an appropriate manner. But a good leader knows the hearts of those they lead and allows that knowledge to overrule any offence that was not intended to be there.

There is a scene in the film *King Arthur*, starring Clive Owen,[3] where Arthur has to tell the rest of the knights that there is one more mission they must go on before their freedom from Roman rule will be granted. As he explains the details, the knights realise that it is the most dangerous mission they have been asked to take... it is certain that lives will be lost.

Lancelot gets right in the face of his leader, Arthur. He lets him know exactly how he feels about the mission – and Arthur stands there and takes it. There is love in his eyes, but more than that, he knows Lancelot's heart. Arthur knows that Lancelot will be there ready for the mission in the morning, but he loves him enough to let him express how he is feeling. That is what Peter taught me: to know the hearts of those I lead and let that knowledge translate into love and understanding.

On the first night of Beth's chemo, Sharron had taken Beth's older brother, Ben (ten) and her younger sister, Lauren (five) home, and comforted them through the troubles of the day. I spent the night at the hospital. I went and sat in a small kitchen area once Beth fell asleep, and it was there that Peter found me, with my head in my hands and tears in my eyes.

> **As Peter sat beside me I will never forget the peace I felt when he placed his hand on my shoulder.**

Peter never really said much to start with; he never asked me if I blamed God or if I was angry with Him. He knew my heart. He did say one thing, though, that I will always remember... He said it was all going to be OK. I know what he meant; whatever the outcome of Beth's illness was, it would be OK... God can do that: 'We know that in all things God works for the good of those who love him, who have been called according to his purpose' (Romans 8:28).

There are many people in the margins that need a man or woman of God to sit with them in their darkest moments and minister God's peace by listening or simply by resting their hand on their shoulder.

If we are not there for them in their darkest moments, despair and depression are. It's at those times people need to know God cares; and He does, it's just us that refuse to be the channel in which He shows it, by staying away from everyday people in everyday places.

Shaving of the head

I'm used to shaving my head; I have had a shaved head for nearly twenty years. It's not uncommon to see bald men walking around, some bald by choice and others through nature. I remember hearing Tony Campolo say once that you need hormones to grow hair and if they're not doing that then they are doing something else... I think he believed a bald head is a solar panel for a sex machine!

Sinéad O'Connor is probably the most famous bald woman in my world, although she has now grown her hair. Some women look fantastic bald, but I really do understand how hair is so important to a woman or young girl growing up. Short hair or no hair is usually associated with men and boys, and few little girls growing up want to be like a boy.

Our Beth is what her mum and I call a 'girly girl' – in other words, she is a girl who likes girl things, dresses, make-up, long hair and lip gloss. When she was seven, her hair was very light blonde and went down past her shoulders. She would love to wear it in a ponytail, pigtails or just down, and she loved her hair like most little girls do.

It was during her second block of intensive chemo that we noticed her hair was falling out. At first it was hair left on her pillow in the morning, but it quickly became clumps of hair left in her comb or brush.

I remember the day when I looked at her and saw so many bald patches and areas that had really thin hair. She looked like a little old lady... it was time for a dad to do what a dad should never have to do: shave his princess' head.

As Beth leaned over the bath and the buzz of the clippers filled the bathroom air, I encouraged her with how beautiful she was going to look bald, and with no struggle but a peaceful surrender she let me shave off what was left of her beautiful blonde locks.

What happened next took my breath away. As Beth stood up straight, very thin from the drugs she was taking, I was taken aback at how beautiful our little princess was without hair. Her bright blue eyes came to life and put a wonderful smile on her dad's face. I lifted her up and said: 'Look!' as we gazed into the bathroom mirror... 'You look beautiful!'

Sometimes in life, that which we value highly can distract us from seeing real beauty.

Don't let the love of Church distract you from the beauty that lies in the margins.

The local pub or the local church?

Going through cancer as a family has a big impact on everyone. Sharron and I woke up to that fact when a couple of families that were going through the same process we were with Beth ended up breaking up. Mums and Dads struggling to deal with the emotions, hurt, and time demands, just drift apart, fall out of love, relinquish their commitment and promises to one another, and separate.

BBC Radio Sheffield asked me to go and do a short interview one Sunday morning about being a minister and having a daughter suffering with cancer. The interviewer that day kept pushing me to say that I doubted God now, or that I was angry with Him, but what I remember saying was something that I hadn't thought of before or prepared beforehand. I asked him, 'When you crush a grape, what do you get?' He replied, 'Grape juice.' 'That's correct,' I replied. 'If you crush a grape you get out what is inside it... it's the same if you crush a man of God... crush him and what will come out of him is God.' And 'God is love' (1 John 4:8).

Not only do we respond when life crushes us, but those around us do also. How does your local church respond when one of the church family goes through a crushing experience? I heard first-hand from a guy whose wife was diagnosed with breast cancer and had to give up work. His local church, his Christian family, got together and bought a big freezer to put in their garage and filled it with meals that the church family cooked, and food that was easy and quick to prepare. Believe me, the last thing you want to do when you have been in hospital all day is come home and figure out what to make the family for their tea.

We should have such a close Christian community that when life crushes one of us, the love of God comes out of those around them.

By this all men will know that you are my disciples, if you love one another. (John 13:35)

One of the fathers that I got to know down at the hospital shared with me one day what his local pub did for them as a family. Now, a lot of local pubs in the UK are like churches in the way that you see the same people in there each time you go, and over a period of time they become your friends. He told me how the landlord (that's the guy who runs the pub... like a pastor who runs a church) decided to have a pub fun day one Saturday to raise money so that his family, who also had a daughter in chemo for leukaemia, could have a holiday at Disney in Florida when they were finished with their treatment... all expenses paid.

A group of people, a community hurting along with a family and choosing to respond in love... Unless you have been in a similar situation, it's hard to really appreciate what a holiday at Disney in Florida can do for a family when they are struggling through chemo, especially for the child who is suffering.

Our kids had always wanted to go to Disney, so when Beth got sick we told her to look forward to going because we were going to take her when she had finished her treatment. To have something like that to look forward to is a great motivator for a child and the family... knowing they have a reward coming and one where the whole family can create memories and history together. It's that potential that is threatened, the potential to create more memories together and take more family pictures.

I was touched by the love of his local pub landlord and of those who all attended the fun day and raised the money for this family's trip.

We were also touched by the family who brought Beth Winnie the Pooh dressed as an angel the first Christmas she was sick. He was especially made to sit on the top of the Christmas tree, and each year he does, and each year we remember that family who showed us love. Sharron had to give up work as soon as Beth started chemo, and going from a two-salary family to one was hard financially, but while we were being crushed so were a couple of families in our church, who posted some money through our letter box to help us through.

If we could take this love... the 'Great Love', and spread it through the margins, can you imagine how many lives would be changed? Or maybe if we spent time in the margins we would be changed by the love we find there.

A knight's tale

I love movies; I find God speaks to me through music and movies more than anything else... apart from my wife, that is!

One of Beth's and my favourite movies is *A Knight's Tale* starring the late Heath Ledger. It's a great tale of how a young peasant boy becomes a knight and world champion at jousting, while conquering his arch-enemy to win the love of a beautiful maiden.

There are so many great scenes: one of them is when Sir William's herald goes out and warms up the crowd before William meets his next jousting opponent. He is introduced by the herald, saying:

My lords, my ladies, and everybody else here not sitting on a cushion! Today... today, you find yourselves equals. For you are all equally blessed. For I have the pride, the privilege, nay, the pleasure of introducing to you to a knight, sired by knights. A knight who can trace his lineage back beyond Charlemagne. I first met him atop a mountain near Jerusalem, praying to God, asking His forgiveness for the Saracen blood spilt by his sword. Next, he amazed me still further in Italy when he saved a fatherless beauty from the would-be ravishing of her dreadful Turkish uncle. In Greece he spent a year in silence just to better understand the sound of a whisper. And so without further gilding the lily and with no more ado, I give to you, the seeker of serenity, the protector of Italian virginity, the enforcer of our Lord God, the one, the only, Sir Ulrich von Lichtenstein![4]

Can you imagine introducing the sermon on Sunday morning like that? Now, that would either be fun – or the end of life as you know it! As the herald walks off the field he looks up at William and says these words:

'I have won their attention; now go win their hearts.'

The first time Beth went into theatre for a lumbar puncture after her chemo had started, she had a dream. In the recovery room after the procedure, Sharron and I were looking over Beth's bed, and when she woke up she told us that she had had a dream when she was put to sleep. Now the dream is a little funny, as dreams usually are, but this is what our little princess dreamt: she dreamt that Mum was a queen and her brother, Ben, was a king, that her sister, Lauren, was a princess like she was and that I was a knight.

A knight in shining armour... I liked that... I liked that a lot.

Beth was going to have lumbar punctures in theatre on a regular basis, so I got on the phone to a friend of mine called Ben Walker, who is a master on eBay, and asked him to look for a knight's helmet for me. Later that same day Ben gave me a call and said he had found a knight's helmet which was a replica of Sir William's in *A Knight's Tale*.

> A few days later my knight's helmet arrived ready for the purpose that it was purchased for.

From that moment on, when Beth was in theatre, I would arrive at the hospital with her, carrying my knight's helmet under my arm, and then when it was time for her to go to theatre I would wear it as we pushed her bed towards the operating room. Then when she was taken into recovery I would be waiting for her to wake up by looking over her bed wearing my knight in shining armour's helmet... The first time I did this the rest of the nurses dressed Sharron up as a queen, but the only things they could find were kids' dressing-up clothes and a magic wand... I don't think Sharron was very impressed – no one could ever find those clothes again after that day!

'If you win their attention, God will win their hearts.'

If you win people's attention with acts of love... God's love... their hearts will be won.

Whoever has your heart has your life.

The problem is when we don't spend time around people who need to have their hearts won by 'The Great Love'... you will be surprised how many people are looking for a knight in shining armour.

Cancer is a barking dog, but love shuts it up.

BAD
LANGUAGE

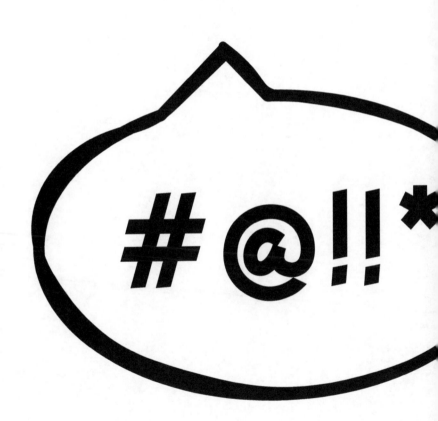

Chapter Six: Bad Language?

The 'F' bomb

Have you ever heard someone say, 'He/she never uses bad language (swears) around me because they know I'm a Christian?'

Maybe it's a generational thing, but I would rather people swear when I'm around, if that is how they usually communicate.

Bad language can so often become a barking dog in our lives; we can easily take offence when we hear people swear and when doing so we step away from them, making the choice that their chosen way to communicate will have no place in our lives, resulting in us avoiding them. Another channel of God's love blocked.

Language fascinates me. I am constantly amazed by how a word in one country can mean something very different in another. How a fag in England is a cigarette, but in the USA it is a derogatory term for a homosexual person.

There are some words that cross cultures and languages. The 'F' word is one of them. You know what word I mean, it is often classified as the most offensive word in the English language. It's the word that if you used it at the dinner table, your mum would probably have a choking fit and your young brother would go around the house saying it from then onwards.

The 'F' word can often be heard in the context of sex, violence, displeasure, threats, surprise and to describe a person's actions with someone's mother.

The 'F' word is often bleeped or dubbed out on cable and satellite channels in the USA and usually bleeped out on TV in the UK before 9pm. The bleep can actually turn some movies into silent movies.

There have been times when I've been chatting with a group of people and someone has used the 'F' word – it has been a conversation stopper... I guess this is where the 'F' word gets the title the 'F' bomb.

There are other 'F' words in the English language that have the same effect, but not the same consequences.

'F'orgiven

'F'orgiveness

'F'orgive

These 'F' words are even more powerful that the 'F' bomb, but unfortunately not spoken as often.

There was a man who walked this earth who used these words often and backed them up with his lifestyle and actions.

He talked about sex, violence, displeasure and harmful living. He let humankind know that there is no sexual act that you can't be forgiven for. There is no violent act towards yourself or others that you can't receive forgiveness for. The displeasure we have with ourselves because we have created a life built on our own foundations and dreams, and the fact that we often take our displeasure out on the world around us, only highlights the need for us to forgive those who hurt and use us, as well as ourselves.

May you from this moment on, when hearing the 'F' word, which will probably be most days of your life, be reminded of Jesus' 'F' bombs – forgiven, forgiveness, forgive – and live with such conviction that they flow out of your mouth and are displayed through your actions.

> **Oh, and don't allow anyone to bleep you...
> or your life could be a silent one!**

Bastard (living an illegitimate lifestyle)

It's a harsh-sounding word isn't it? There is nothing endearing or beautiful about the way this word sounds, and in this day and age it is usually used to describe an unpleasant or despicable person, often a male.

In some parts of London, 'bastard' can be used as a term of endearment between men... so and so is a 'proper bastard' actually means that the man being spoken about is a good friend, loyal, a person you would stand by and who would stand by you. But call the same man a 'bastard' and it means the complete opposite.

Originally 'bastard' was a derogatory name given to a child who was born outside of marriage. In many cases today when a child is born outside of marriage they often grow up with little or no contact with their father. Fortunately today they are not branded with such a hurtful name.

Another name used for bastard is 'illegitimate'. Meaning the same, that a child has been born outside of marriage and has an absent father.

Living an illegitimate lifestyle, a fatherless lifestyle, and a life with no contact or little contact with the father that conceived you can have dramatic effects on a person's life.

I have worked with and met many young men who do not know their father, or have very little contact with him. They often carry a real wound that displays itself through abusive behaviour towards themselves and others, carrying a void, a longing for something that they may not know how to describe but is there because they have missed a vital relationship in their life.

Having a father and being fathered are two different things

As I have grown up in this crazy world I have been blessed to have a good father. My dad worked hard to put food on the table. I remember days when I was a kid, my dad coming home from a long day at work and then doing extra jobs outside of his regular one so we would not go without. I have also discovered in this life my heavenly Father whose love is unconditional and who wants to see the desires of my heart come into being.

I have two fathers... an earthly one and a heavenly one.

But I have a choice... will I live an illegitimate lifestyle, will I become a bastard by not allowing my fathers to father me?

I know you may not have a choice today as to whether or not your earthly father will father you, but you do have a choice in whether or not you will allow your heavenly Father to father you.

You have a choice to become a legitimate son or daughter of your heavenly Father, carrying no longer the void that an absent father leaves in your life. You can live knowing the Father's love, care, guidance and discipline. I know 'discipline' is a word we like to hide from, but a father who deeply loves only gives true loving discipline. We grow better for it.

Maybe today you have never given thought to your heavenly Father, even doubting that He exists or cares? Has He been silent in your life up to now? Has He been absent? Or could it be, you just haven't been listening for His voice or looking out for His presence? Either way it doesn't change the fact that your Father in heaven is desperate to be in contact with His distant sons and daughters.

Or maybe you know your heavenly Father and are enjoying His care. I ask only one question: if a stranger was to observe you today, watching your actions and listening to your words, what conclusion would they come to? Would they see you as one who is fathered, or as a bastard?

'Our souls' shall sing

Church services can be incredibly boring and stale, but they can also be very entertaining.

I have attended more church services in my lifetime than I can count, but there is one that stands out above the rest, simply because it was one of the funniest moments in my life.

Let me start the story by painting the scene. It was March 2006, in Sheffield. A great team of young men and women and I were hosting a youth conference called TRUTH06. The conference was to be attended by teenagers and leaders of all denominations from across the city and the UK.

We had a great band leading the worship, which included Andy Baker (who is a music producer and songwriter), Nick Noble (who is the frontman for The Gentlemen and a lyrical genius), Mandy Toombs (who is part of a great trio called Golddigger), Joel Hanna (drummer and husband to Philippa), Josh Cana (currently the bass player for The Human League), Sean D'Souza Walsh (lead guitarist from The Gentlemen), Nick Law (keyboard player and songwriter) and Philippa Hanna (singer and songwriter).

Our guest speaker that day was the Archbishop of York, John Sentamu, the first black Archbishop in the Church of England. Brother John is an amazingly humble man and it was a real honour to have him with us as our guest that day.

The day went really well with hundreds in attendance and various seminars and workshops taking place. The evening arrived and brought with it a great atmosphere as even more piled into the building for the final service of the day.

There is something very special when a large crowd of people gather together with an expectancy and energy for worship... it's electric.

The band was on form. They started playing and the area in front of the stage filled up with teenagers hungry to show their passion in worship.

So... I was sitting on the front row next to the archbishop and we were surrounded by teenagers dancing, jumping and passionately worshiping God. Nick, the frontman for The Gentlemen, is a real character; he is one of those rare people that has a great stage presence and the talent to go with it. There have been times that I have heard him sing and wonder if heaven would have anything better.

Nick started to lead the crowd in a song that has the refrain 'my soul, my soul will sing', but as the whole crowd were singing with him he decided to change one of the words, which changed everything...

Nick began to sing 'our souls' will sing, over and over, and everyone joined in, the crowd down the front, everyone else in their seats, the archbishop and myself.

Then it dawned on me what we were singing, you see... 'our souls, our souls will sing', when sung with an English accent actually sounds like 'arse holes, arse holes will sing'!

I had a bunch of skater kids next to me with their hands held high, singing with all their passion 'arse holes, arse holes will sing'!

I had the band in front of me trying to keep their composure as they led the crowd in a song about the miracle of your butt singing!

I had the Archbishop of York, the second most senior cleric in the Church of England, standing with me singing 'arse holes, arse holes will sing'!

It took me a long time to gather my composure as tears were running down my face, and my sides were hurting so much from laughing that I thought I was going to wet myself!

I often think back to that moment and wonder if heaven laughed? I know one thing: I wish church was that funny all the time – laughter truly is good medicine.

I hope today this story has cheered you up, and be encouraged – for it is only in church that the miracle of 'arse holes' singing will take place.

Praise the LORD, O my soul; all my inmost being, praise his holy name. (Psalm 103:1)

Two-finger salute

Two fingers raised, your middle finger and index finger with the rest folded downwards, with the back of your hand facing the subject.

In America this gesture means 'peace' but in the UK it is the equivalent to giving somebody the bird (which is the showing of just the middle finger).

The two-finger salute, as it has become known, is used when expressing displeasure with someone. It's a sign of defiance which traces its origins back to the Battle of Agincourt which was a part of the Hundred Years' War.

The French soldiers would catch the English archers and cut off the two fingers which they used to draw back their bow. So the English would taunt them by waving their two fingers in the air. This is also where the middle finger gesture, which is more commonly used in America, gets its name 'The Bird', which is in relation to the bird feathers that were used on an archer's arrows.

Winston Churchill used the two-finger salute to represent V for victory during the Second World War. It became a sign that brought much inspiration and instilled much courage into a nation that was experiencing its darkest hour. V for victory over the enemy became a symbol that is still used today all over the world.

US President Richard Nixon used it to signal victory (with the palm of the hand facing outwards), an act that became one of his best-known trademarks. One that he used in his departure from public office in 1974.

In street language the giving of the two-finger salute simply means 'f#@! off'.

I find the two-finger salute inspirational for two reasons; first because it means victory and second because it is a gesture of defiance.

As a Christian I believe in the forces of good and evil. I believe in the power of the devil and the divine power of God. I understand that I am in an eternal struggle between right and wrong, both within myself and in life in general.

I fight within to do the right thing, to make the right decisions, to have the right attitude so I can be victorious over selfishness. I fight to make life better for those around me, the ones I know by name and the ones I don't. I am gonna hold my two-finger salute up to the devil and his team in defiance and victory, like my forefathers.

Shadrach, Meshach and Abednego held up their two-finger salutes while being thrown into the flames.

Daniel held up his two-finger salute when praying with the window open after the anti-prayer law was passed.

David held up his two-finger salute when faced with a man much greater than himself.

Joseph held up his two-finger salute while not giving in to sexual temptation.

Job held up his two-finger salute while suffering in ways he had previously never imagined.

Paul held up his two-finger salute during his beatings, hunger, misunderstanding and attempts on his life.

Jesus held up His two-finger salute while being nailed to the cross and choosing to stay there until His work was done.

Choose this day to take your stand, to stand boldly for truth, to right the wrongs that are around you. And as you do you will find others joining in, raising their two-finger salute in defiance of poverty, crime and injustice. Together pressing on through the dark to see a victory that will bring a glorious renewing!

I salute you!

What the bleep!

Do you recognise any of these movie lines?

What the bleep!

Bleep off!

Bleep you!

Oh bleep!

I don't give a bleep!

The famous bleep, or a moment of dubbed silence to cover over a swear word, is done by TV stations all over the world. There are a number of reasons why they feel it necessary to bleep out these words. They may be obeying a law, such as in the UK where regular TV shows cannot contain offensive language before 9pm, or it could be for religious reasons.

Not only do TV stations bleep out swear words, but they can also delete whole scenes from a movie if they deem the scene to be too violent or sexual. I was watching a Mel Gibson film the other day on TV in which a whole scene was deleted (it was the one where a not so very nice man takes a hammer to Mel's feet). But if you didn't know about the scene you would be left with a question for the rest of the movie: why the heck is Mel limping so badly?

As a man who holds a deep faith in God – not religion, but faith in a God who created everything and everyone for a reason, a God who loves unconditionally, and is able to help us through the many tragedies of life, a God who communicates to us, and a God who loves for us to communicate to Him – I have noticed an increasing anger in society towards Christianity.

It's a mad world we live in when you can be as vulgar, rude, obscene, offensive as you would like to be and become famous for it. But if you speak out about injustice and you are a Christian you are bleeped out and people try to delete the scene of your life out of history. Then they ask the question when a tragedy takes place either personally or nationally: what has caused us to limp like this?

If only they hadn't deleted or bleeped out the voice that often cries out in the wilderness, then they would understand who took hold of the hammer and why.

We do know why the hammer was taken hold of that drove those nails into Jesus' hands and feet. The religious system wanted to delete His life and bleep out His words... but not even death could stop truth from rising.

I hope you discover the beauty of the 'F' word, receiving and giving forgiveness; don't let anyone bleep you when you use the 'F' words that Jesus used!

I also hope that you will receive revelation concerning you being a son/daughter of God...

> ## ...who is also your heavenly Father.
> ## He has no bastard children!

I thank you for standing with the millions that have gone before us and with the ones that are now and those who will follow in our footsteps as disciples. Let's give the two-finger salute of defiance and victory together!

May our souls sing on that great and glorious day when we are rewarded for not allowing anyone to bleep our words of love and justice and for standing strong and fighting the good fight of faith... refusing to allow the delete button to be pushed.

What we do in life echoes in eternity.
Marcus Aurelius – *Gladiator*

My dear children, let's not just talk about love; let's practice real love. This is the only way we'll know we're living truly, living in God's reality. It's also the way to shut down debilitating self-criticism, even when there is something to it. For God is greater than our worried hearts and knows more about us than we do ourselves. (1 John 3:18–20, *The Message*)

25
YEARS
AND
COUNTING

~~HHH~~ ~~HHH~~ ~~HHH~~

~~HHH~~ ~~HHH~~

Chapter Seven: 25 Years and Counting

In the end, we will remember not the words of our enemies, but the silence of our friends.

Martin Luther King, Jr

Your friendships can bring you so much joy and so much pain.

There is not a person alive who has not been hurt, wounded and scarred because of a relationship they have had. It could have been an abusive or absent parent, a bad schoolteacher, a disloyal friend, a cruel boss or work colleagues, an overbearing pastor, a cheating spouse or partner, a breakdown in relationship with your child.

We can also receive wounds through good relationships. When a terminal illness takes your child, when aging parents pass away, when a loved one dies in an accident or act of war.

It is not that these relationships set out to hurt you, but that your love allowed you to take the risk and enjoy the journey while trusting and not knowing how each relationship would work out.

We can only truly discover ourselves through the relationships we have. We learn so much about ourselves as we walk through life with our good and bad relationships. We uncover what our motives are, how forgiving we are, or are not. We discover what compels us to love, what drives us to hate, what moves us to tears and what inspires us to change.

I have seen in my own life how relationships are seasonal. Sometimes you move and have to make friends all over again; other times your friends move and leave a gap in your life; you leave a place of education, join a new church, change your local pub – all of these will bring a change of friendships.

When I lived in America I found three great friends.

Wes was the manager of the 'Carolina Ale House' that became my local (I didn't drink alcohol while on staff at the church I was working at, as that was one of the requirements of pastoral staff members). He was football mad (that's soccer for my American friends), which instantly gave us some common ground. I would often hear Wes say that he would love to play recreational soccer for a living.

Chris was another friend my life was graced with. Chris is a hunk of man with a solid frame and was the captain of the high school football team (that's American football, which is like rugby but with health and safety). Chris is all-American; he runs his own business and loves to ride his Harley on warm summer days. He has a big heart and values family; he is one of those guys that if you ever have to go to war, you would want a man like Chris next to you.

Bob is probably the tallest man I know and the most laid back. He is the district youth director in South Carolina. I actually met Bob on my very first visit to America. He was due to pick me up from Columbia airport in South Carolina, but went to Charlotte airport in North Carolina. Arriving late in the evening in a strange place and not knowing anyone was an experience! I tried calling his office once I'd found a hotel to stay in for the night, but the answerphone hadn't been turned on.

We eventually got in touch with each other early the following morning and as soon as I met Bob, I knew I had a friend for life. This brother has been a true friend to me. We still meet up most years when Bob comes over for a few days to Sheffield to enjoy Match Day at Sheffield United. The funny thing is, all the regulars in the pub pull a face when he walks in, because every time he has gone to the match, we have never won!

Bob has taught me a lot over the past twenty years. He has a bucket full of wisdom which he regularly shares with me when we talk about life. But I have learned just as much from him by observing his actions. He is a man with a heart for people and full of compassion.

Each of us have different personalities, but we had different journeys that brought us together in the same town for a season. Although Wes now lives in Florida, Chris and Bob in South Carolina and myself in England, we have found a brotherhood and common bond that has empowered us to take a risk on each other; we had to trust each other. We all needed guys in our lives who we could share the good, the bad and the ugly with, while knowing we would each be spurred on to be better, and not judged for being human.

> **I have discovered so much about myself because of their friendships**

When I have doubted my gifts and talents, they have relentlessly encouraged me when they could so easily have walked away. I recovered an inner strength and sense of purpose. They have corrected me at times, not in a way that made them feel better for putting me down, but in a way that gave me hope and self-belief.

Wounds from a sincere friend are better than many kisses from an enemy. (Proverbs 27:6, NLT)

When I needed my true friends, they didn't let me down. They especially stood with me side by side as I went through the transition of moving back to England. They went through the heartbreak with me and I will never forget that, their love and brotherhood kept me going through my darkest time.

Sharron and I returned to South Carolina after eighteen months of being back in England and the great thing was that when we met up with Chris and his wife, Joanna, and Bob and his wife, Michelle, it was like we had never been apart.

I reckon that's how people like Lazarus, Mary, Martha and others felt when they met up with Jesus from time to time: accepted, loved, trusted, and as if they had never been apart.

Love at first sight

> **Do you believe in 'love at first sight'?**

'Love at first sight', seeing a person and knowing that you will die before you stop dedicating your love to him/her each and every day of your life here on earth.

I remember seeing Sharron (my wife of twenty-five years) for the first time in the summer of 1990. It was 'love at first sight'. I had some life experience by this point and I knew without a shadow of a doubt that I wanted to be with her forever.

I was visiting my cousin David, who was a pastor at a church in Grimsby, and his wife, Ann Marie. While waiting for the evening service to start I noticed Sharron walk in. She was with a guy who I later found out was just a friend. I can honestly say, my heart skipped a beat when I set my eyes on her. All during the service I kept looking over at her – a bit stalker-ish, I know, but I was going to get to meet this beautiful young woman if it was the last thing I did.

After church, a young couple invited all the young adults around to their house for supper. There were a lot of people there that night and the house was rather full. I remember sitting on the floor having a deep conversation about faith with a guy when something happened which had not happened to me before. It was like God had turned up the volume and spoke to me at the top of His voice: 'The one behind you is the one you are going to marry.'

About eighteen months before this I had made the decision that I wasn't going to date anyone unless I felt they were the right one for me, and me for them.

I am so pleased that when I glanced around to see who was sitting behind me that it was a woman – and that woman was Sharron!

I am a very impulsive person, but on this occasion I thought it would be best to ask this young woman's name first before I jumped straight in and asked her to marry me. So I turned round (after all, chatting to Sharron was going to be a lot more fun than chatting to the guy I was sitting with) and said, 'Hi, my name is Andy.' Love had got me; every word that we spoke to each other that evening just filled me with joy and excitement.

That evening when returning back to David and Ann Marie's house, we got talking about Sharron. Ann Marie told me that Sharron lived just around the corner in the nursing flats at Grimsby hospital, where she was in her final year of training.

The next morning I got up early and went downstairs to get some breakfast. Ann Marie was in the kitchen and she said to me, 'I've called Sharron and she is coming over at 10am for morning coffee.' I just smiled, but inside I was shouting, 'Get in!'

Sharron arrived and we sat in the living room. Ann Marie brought coffee and cake, then said, 'I've got things to do so I'll leave you both to it.' We talked about all kinds of things as we started to get to know each other. After a few hours, we decided to go to a small seaside town, Cleethorpes, which was just a few miles away. We played crazy golf and went for a walk around the boating lake.

I had to travel home that evening, which was about 100 miles away. That was a long way back then, we had no mobile phones or computers, so the only way we could keep in contact was by writing letters and calling each other from a payphone.

The following Saturday I travelled up to see Sharron again; this was our second date. Sharron put together a nice ham salad lunch and after we had eaten I decided to get straight to the point.

I shared my dreams with Sharron: what I believed God had given me life for, how I believed that we would both complement each other in our life callings, and how I fancied her and wanted to kiss her forever. After that was all said, I asked her to marry me and she said yes! We kissed and the adventure began.

One year and one week from meeting we got married. My cousin David did the service; Sharron stole the day; family and friends celebrated with us both. So far we have enjoyed twenty-five years of marriage. One of the greatest compliments that we can receive is when we are complimented on our relationship and marriage. In this day and age more people are watching you in your marriage than you realise. We are all looking for hope in a world where divorce is too common an experience for so many.

> Who can find a virtuous and capable wife?
>
> She is more precious than rubies.
>
> Her husband can trust her,
>
> and she will greatly enrich his life.
>
> She brings him good, not harm,
>
> all the days of her life. (Proverbs 31:10–12, NLT)

Truth!

Here is a question for all the men: 'Have you ever tried on a dress?'

When reading the Bible you will come across the picture of the Church as a bride… Jesus' bride. Now, I am a believer in Jesus and I am part of the universal Church, but as a guy it is sometimes hard to imagine myself as a bride!

If Jesus was to see His future bride (the Church) for the first time, would He experience 'love at first sight'? Would Jesus be swept away in romance by how beautiful she looks? When observing the way she moved and the places she would go, would He be compelled to follow her? While listening to her words, would He be swept away with how she displayed her inner beauty? Would He be moved to whisper words of love into her ear and shower her with affection?

If you bumped into Jesus today in your town or city, would He find a friend that would stick with Him closer than any brother (see Proverbs 18:24)?

> **Could the problem with religion, Christianity and the Church be us? You and I?**

Could it be that we heard Jesus share His dream with us, but we haven't allowed His love to bring out the best in us?

How does the Church (the bride) look to those outside?

Where is the bride willing to go to share her love?

Are people swept away with love when they hear the Church's (bride's) words?

I want to be loved at first sight and Jesus wants to love the Church at first sight, so maybe you and I need to make some changes and get ready for a new kind of romance.

I have purposely not written about all my bad experiences with people who have confessed friendship to me, but then by their actions and words have treated me like an enemy or something that gets stuck to the bottom of their shoe.

Those barking dogs have been shut up by the love of brothers and a good woman. I've still got the scars, but the healing is the beauty of this message.

Never stop searching for 'The Great Love'. God is not hiding.

THE FULL
MONTY

Chapter Eight: The Full Monty

Dave: 'Anti-wrinkle cream there may be, but anti-fat-bastard cream there is none.'

Don't be fools; be wise: make the most of every opportunity you have for doing good. (Ephesians 5:16, TLB)

The Full Monty is a 1997 British comedy about six unemployed Sheffield steel workers who form a male striptease act, cheered on by women to go for 'the full Monty'.

There is nothing funny about being unemployed, especially when you have a family to provide for. It can bring a man to his all-time low.

One evening I was having a pint with some mates of mine, Mark (record dealer), Neil (ice skate blade designer, baker and brewer), Jon (retired technician) and Bob (who worked in the snooker club we owned). We were laughing about *The Full Monty* and some of the many funny scenes in the film and at Mark who insisted that he looked like the lead actor, Robert Carlyle.

I love sitting with these fellas and talking about life, along with the rubbish that men can chat about while having a drink.

We all have stories and experiences that each of us can relate to. Cancer is one of those things that at some point has affected us all either directly or indirectly.

I'm not sure how the conversation came around, but it was suggested in a very encouraging and positive way, that we could put on a full Monty show in Bar Abbey (which was part of the snooker club) and raise money for a cancer charity.

Now I know what you may be thinking... But let me assure you, we were not drunk, just in high spirits.

Could we pull it off? Would it be the actual full Monty, right down to our birthday suits? Would people pay £10 for a ticket? Would we sell enough? Would people really want to see middle-aged men in the buff? And along with all those questions that were flying across the table, the biggest one was yet to come: 'Who is going to teach us how to dance?'

We all went our separate ways that night agreeing in principle that we would do it ... you only live once, right?

> **We set off home to chat to our wives and see if we could get their permission**

Bear this in mind: our ages spread from forty-five to sixty-five, so when asking our wives how they felt if their husbands were to do a show that ended with them being completely naked on stage, the response was not what we were expecting... my Sharron just put a massive smile on her face and then fell about laughing!

The next week when all the fellas got back together, we decided to go for it.

Rehearsals would take place every Monday evening in Bar Abbey. I took on the responsibility of finding security men's costumes which could be pulled off quickly and bright red underpants that had Velcro fastenings on the side so they could be pulled off easily. I was also given the responsibility of sorting out advertising.

The only person we were now missing was someone who could control five men at rehearsals (which was not going to be easy) and bring choreography that five fellas with little rhythm could pull off. This is where Amy came in.

Amy was a creative woman who had recently put on an event in Bar Abbey and sold it out. She had a great manner about her; she was firm, direct, and knew what she was doing when it came to putting a show together.

Amy didn't take much persuading when I asked her to consider helping us; after she stopped laughing (and then laughing some more) she graciously agreed to be involved as the director of the show.

We decided that we would do three scenes from the film: the auditions that took place in an abandoned warehouse, the 'dole queue' scene, and the final dance, ending in the full Monty. We also asked some acts if they would do individual slots: a magician, a Michael Jackson impersonator, some bands etc., and we found a great young comedian to MC the evening.

My good friend Revd Harry Steele said that he would help out behind the bar, as did Sharron. The night was shaping up to be a fantastic event. After many discussions we decided to give the proceeds raised from the evening to a charity that helped men who had been diagnosed with testicular cancer; a good cause, right?

Rehearsals start

We started rehearsing in September and the show was going to take place the following March. This gave us plenty of time to shape up and learn our routines.

I can't really put into words how much laughter we had during these Monday nights while learning the choreography; it really did prove the point that white men can't dance, but with much practice, sweat and tears, we started to shape up rather nicely.

One thing that will always stay in my memories is Mark on those Monday nights. Mark found out that one of his local pubs sold a large selection of beer for £1.50 a pint on Mondays, so he would often turn up to rehearsals very merry, and when Mark is merry his concentration span is almost zero. Amy really had her work cut out trying to control him.

I eventually sourced the costumes and the evening soon arrived for our first dress rehearsal... This was not going to be a pretty sight.

Being naked with four other men is not something I do regularly, you will be pleased to know. It was going to be a challenge for all of us to get used to taking our clothes off in front of each other. We were all different shapes and sizes.

I remember Mark coming to rehearsal one night and getting us all laughing...

...when he told us his neighbour had caught him in the garden doing star jumps in his Y-fronts...

...because he wanted to get in better shape!

As five brave men, we just got on with it. I can honestly say I never thought I would get used to having a bare man's bum stuck in my face while trying to pick up my clothes after a dress rehearsal, but it soon became second nature. Trying to make sure we picked up the right pair of undies was a constant challenge.

Late on during one rehearsal, Amy suggested that we put another final scene in. When I purchased the rip-off trousers they came with a silver thong, cuffs and a collar. Amy thought it would be a great end to the show if, after the full Monty scene, we all put these on with our boots and came out for a question and answer session with the audience.

I was trying to imagine this as she was talking: black boots, a silver thong, cuffs and a collar. We were going to look like waiters in a saucy club for women of a certain age! But hey... at least we'd have something on. So we all agreed and the surprise for me was that this was to turn out to be the best part of the evening.

Tickets go on sale

Posters went up in local shops, pubs, work canteens and in the snooker club. Tickets went on sale, and we had 150 to sell which would take the venue to capacity.

BBC Radio Sheffield got wind of what we were doing and asked if they could send a reporter down to one of our rehearsals to interview us. This would then be played at intervals throughout the day and evening shows advertising the event. This really boosted our confidence – could this really be a sell-out?

To our surprise it didn't take long till we SOLD OUT! The pressure was really on now: we wanted to raise a good amount of money for our chosen charity, but we also wanted to put on a good show, as professional as we could. Rehearsals were going really well and we had even surprised ourselves with how good we had become. It probably goes without saying, but I'll say it anyway... virtually all the tickets were purchased by women.

As the time drew near for the Saturday night show, we squeezed in a few extra rehearsals, making sure all our timings were spot on, and we had all the details covered. I've got to say, I think all of us were getting a little nervous with imagining 150 women in front of us as we danced and took off our uniforms. Even though all of our wives were going to be there cheering us on, it was something none of us had done before.

Show time

The day had finally arrived. I remember getting up that Saturday morning feeling both excited and nervous, along with a huge sense of achievement. I was very proud of the fellas that I had been on this journey with. Our friendship had grown so deep as we faced personal challenges together, encouraging each other every step of the way. There were times when as individuals we had doubts, but our friendship and the fact we were doing something worthwhile kept us going right up to the end. This fellowship of men were true friends.

The other acts started to turn up early for their sound checks. The room was set, bar staff were in position and the dressing room off the side of the stage was prepared. It was now time to open the doors, and to my surprise when doing so, there was already a queue of ladies waiting.

The place started to fill up fast until there was no more room, it really was a full house. Music playing before the show seemed to calm our nerves and it didn't seem long until the audience were enjoying the opening act... the atmosphere was electric.

We coped well with our first two scenes which were sandwiched between other acts, and then the time came for the full Monty scene. I remember being in the dressing room with the fellas, putting on our red undies and then our security guard uniforms and finally our hats... we looked great.

It was my privilege to go out and address the audience before the music started. I spoke about how proud I was of the fellas and the journey we had all been on. I talked about how much we hate cancer and how we decided to fight back. I asked if nobody would take pictures or video as we all had kids and didn't want our performance plastered all over social media.

Here we go! I stopped talking, gave the sound man the nod and the music started... 'You Can Keep Your Hat On'... there was no going back now.

As each of us took our place and started dancing, the noise was immense, with 150 women clapping, cheering, singing and whistling. All was good as I made eye contact with Sharron in the front of the crowd.

Every step was in time, just as we had rehearsed so many times before that night. The jacket came off, then the tie (which was thrown into the crowd) and shirt, the belt was taken off slowly and waved around in the air before we let go of it. The trousers pulled off just as we planned and were thrown into the crowd... that left us with our boots, red pants and hats on.

The hats came off our heads and we held them in front of... well, you know where. We pulled off our red pants one side at a time and then just as the song finished we threw our hats in the air... and that's the full Monty standing before you!

The lights went out, we shuffled into the dressing room and just hugged each other... we had done it! We could still hear the crowd cheering – what a buzz and great sense of achievement and relief flooded over us all.

The final part

We still had one more part to do... it was time to put on the silver thongs, collar and cuffs and go out to answer some questions.

I said earlier that this would turn out to be my favourite moment and that was for two reasons.

Firstly, as we all walked back onto the stage and stood in a straight line ready to answer questions, I noticed that Jon, who was the oldest one in the cast, had put on his silver thong back to front... the big bit was over his bum and the small bit... well, let's just say it didn't cover what it was meant to cover! :-0 We all still laugh about this today.

As the questions were being asked and the microphone passed between us to give answers, a lady asked me a question: 'How do you deal with being a reverend and taking your clothes off in a show?'

This was my opportunity!

Whenever I have to speak in public, if it's a speech at a birthday party or at one of Sharron's and my wedding anniversary parties, I seize the opportunity to share the great message of the gospel and God's love for us all.

I'm not sure what came over me as I was handed the microphone to give an answer, but it was God-inspired. With confidence and authority I said, 'If our Lord and Saviour Jesus Christ can give up His life, be stripped naked, beaten then hung on a cross to die so that we could live knowing God's forgiveness and love, then I can take my clothes off in a show and raise money for a charity that lets men who are battling cancer know that they are loved and supported.'

The response in the room once I had finished speaking will stay with me all my life. Everybody just cheered and started to clap... God filled that room that night; I seized the opportunity and God spoke.

My mate Revd Harry who had been serving at the bar came up to me afterwards and said, 'I never thought I would see the day when a man dressed in a silver thong and boots would bring the gospel message to a room full of women.'

It was a bizarre moment, but the gospel was preached, albeit briefly, to a room where it was needed and received.

God truly does move in mysterious ways!

DON'T
LOSE
HEART

Chapter Nine: Don't Lose Heart

From personal experience I have learned some valuable lessons when it comes to not losing heart. The Bible says that the heart is 'the wellspring of life', so we must guard our hearts above all else (Proverbs 4:23).

You know what it is like when you start to lose heart in a relationship, job, project, yourself or the Church. Fear can creep in, vision is watered down and listening to the lies of the enemy weakens us.

You and I were created in God's image, to do the work of God. He planned a specific journey for each of us, each step planned, each relationship marked out, and He gave us faith to trust in Him and in His provision.

If we lose heart in who we are in God and what He has created us to do, life will become mundane, restricted and not what we dreamed of when we were much younger or when we first became a follower of Christ.

I hope by sharing some very personal experiences with you and truth that I have discovered in the Word of God, that you may discover areas in your life in which the enemy has got in and caused you to lose heart. You may be surprised by how he does this; he is a crafty so-and-so, that father of lies.

Who are you listening to?

When you find yourself in a place that looks like a dead end, stuck with nowhere to go, no horizon to look at and darkness resting upon you like a heavy wet blanket, it's hard to believe there is anything good for you anymore... you lose heart in all that you believed, all that you dreamed and in those relationships that you placed your trust in.

You can find yourself in a place like this when you listen to people's negative perceptions about you

Israel, travelling through the desert looking for the land that had been promised to them by God, made this fatal mistake.

When the spies came back from taking a secret look at the Promised Land, all but two of them gave a report that there were giants in the land and the people of Israel were like grasshoppers; they would never be able to overthrow them.

Two of the spies, Joshua and Caleb, saw the same giants and could see that Israel looked like tiny grasshoppers to them, but they listened to God's promise above human negative perceptions. (You will find this story in the book of Numbers, chapter 13).

If you listen to those around you, especially when they act and speak out of jealousy, insecurity and dislike, you will never accomplish what God created you to do and you will never see your dreams come to pass.

Their words are like snake bites, shooting venom into your bloodstream until it reaches your heart and starts to eat away at everything you believed and knew to be true. The sad fact is that the devil will often use Christian brothers and sisters to do this work for him. He knows that if you lose heart you are no longer a threat to the kingdom of darkness.

And if he can use Christian leaders and church members to do this, he is also trying to get you to lose heart in the Church of Jesus Christ.

I have experienced the pain of these venomous snake bites, I have stared at the brick wall, feeling insignificant, and I have felt the heavy darkness. A short time ago I would have just climbed the wall giving a war cry all the way, but listening to human perceptions of yourself steals courage, boldness and passion from you, just as it did to the people of Israel.

I have had human perceptions thrown at me in ways that I have never experienced until recently. They do leave wounds and scars, but one thing I will not allow them to do is steal my dreams, courage, passion and my war cry!

If you are listening to human negative perceptions of yourself above God's, then stop it! Even if they are coming from a parent, pastor or professor. Soak yourself in what God says about you, dream again and pick up your sword... God is cheering your name!

Let the war cry, boldness and courage be unearthed, and let the love of God and His grace and mercy become the antidote to the enemy's venom.

Who is bigger?

> **You will lose heart when your struggles are bigger than your God!**

We all know this but let me say it anyway. No one is exempt from troubles in life. We all have friends and family that pass away, money troubles at times, difficult relationships to work through and sickness to deal with.

It's just part and parcel of being alive; trouble will come to everyone.

A few years ago trouble came to me and my family in a way that we were never expecting. One decision that was out of our control brought unthinkable changes to us.

One decision had a knock-on effect, like dominoes falling. We lost our job, our house, cars, friends, future plans and every penny we had invested. We had to make another international move back to the UK. If you have ever moved internationally then you will know what it takes, physically, emotionally and financially.

But when someone who has authority makes decisions out of your control, it is very important, in fact it is essential, not to lose sight that God is bigger than any one person and their decisions.

It is in times like this that you need to know what kind of God you serve. Is your God one who forgets about you in the days of trouble? Washing His hands of you? Is He a God that has no compassion, no back-up plan and no tears for you?

Or do you serve a God that never stops thinking about you, a God who can't forget about you because you're His son/daughter, and your Saviour is constantly interceding on your behalf? He loves to parade you.

Is your God one who will never wash His hands of you? He may seem silent and distant at times, but that is because He is training your hands for the things He wants of you.

Is your God the Master Creator and the only one who can work in all the good and bad experiences of your life so that they turn out for your good?

You will lose heart when your struggles are bigger than your God.

May this day bring to you a revelation of how big the God you serve really is.

They may take away your house, your car and your clothes, but humans can never take away your God... and our God is bigger than any struggle we are facing and will face!

How big is your God?

He trains my hands for battle; my arms can bend a bow of bronze. (Psalm 18:34)

Listening to negative news reports

Can you remember the last time you sat down to watch the evening news or read the daily newspaper and were overjoyed by what you read and saw?

The only time a smile is usually experienced while watching the news is when the sporting results are reported, and that's only if your team won.

If you listen to the news and then just accept that this is the way the world is, you will lose heart. You will slowly believe that there is no hope for today.

This also happens when you listen to negative reports about yourself. You slowly lose hope in the person you are, and the negative perception of others becomes your reality.

With the effects of global warming, wars and rumours of wars, increasing violence among teenagers and pre-teens, the divorce rate being the same among Christians and non-Christians, the recession and global disasters that claim thousands of lives, it is easy to believe that small insignificant you could never make a difference – and when you believe that, you choose not to make a difference.

It is important that you don't soak your life in the daily news more than the Word of God. The Word of God gives hope in hopeless situations, it inspires you to stand up and make a difference even if you are from a no-name family, have no or little education; and it brings to your life the grace to forgive yourself and others and do all you can to touch one life at a time.

God's report on you is very positive...

...and if you listen to it, soak yourself in it, you will slowly begin to believe it, and when you believe it, it will become your reality.

I am not saying you will become a national figure, preaching to thousands, invited to speak at all the current conferences and high-profile churches. But what will be yours is the joy of knowing that your actions and words each day are constructed in such a way as to bring love and hope into the lives of those around you.

When I arrived back in the city of Sheffield, it would have been easy for me to see all the problems of this city that I have grown to love over the last sixteen years and believe that Church could never make a significant impact there; that the crime rate among teenagers would keep on increasing and that the arts would be used to promote godless instead of godly living.

But today I choose to take heart and listen to what the Word and Spirit of God is saying to me. I am here to make a difference, just like you, so let's not be overcome by the reports on the news and the articles we read in the papers, but let us choose to make a difference right where we are, one act of love at a time and one life at a time.

You have been chosen; you have been called. Turn off the TV, put the newspaper in the cat litter tray and begin to look at what is happening around you through God's eyes.

Take heart!

> Do not lose heart or be afraid when rumours are heard in the land; one rumour comes this year, another the next, rumours of violence in the land and of ruler against ruler. (Jeremiah 51:46)

Do you trust your Father in heaven?

'Discipline' is not a nice word; I don't know anyone who when hearing that word or saying it does so with real joy and excitement.

My wife and I have been blessed with three children, each of them a different personality with their own likes and dislikes. As they were growing up we had to teach them right from wrong and to listen to their parents' voices.

Now, right and wrong when you are a toddler is not a choice between one glass of wine and two bottles of wine or what clothes they should wear or not. When you are young, your parents teach you right from wrong in simple things, like: don't put a banana skin in the video recorder, don't open the baby powder and tip it all over your head; instead put the skin in the bin and leave the baby powder alone.

As we grow up, our choices between what is right and wrong have a bigger impact, both on our own lives and those around us.

We may outlive our earthly parents, but we will never outlive our

Father in heaven. He never abandons us; He is committed to us as we journey through this world, eager to have a healthy father-child relationship with us all. And that means He will have to discipline us at times when we make wrong choices or mistakes.

Now, I know what most people will think when it comes to God's discipline... that He is hard, harsh, cruel and unloving. But that is not the case at all. If we truly trust God, then we will trust Him when He disciplines.

If we didn't trust in our parents' discipline when growing up we would become reckless, undisciplined and, in many cases, hard-hearted.

If we don't trust God and in His discipline for us, then we will lose heart; we will lose heart in a God that works everything around for our good; we will lose heart in a God who is a loving Father and has a great plan for our lives; and if we don't trust God when He disciplines us... we end up losing faith.

God is a perfect Father. He is reaching out to us to teach us, train us, direct us, inspire us, protect us, challenge us and correct us, in order that we don't miss His perfect will for our lives.

May I ask you an honest question? If you have lost heart in God, faith and the Church, is it because God challenged you and corrected you, and like an unruly or proud child, you chose to fight against His discipline? I'm just asking the question, not pointing any fingers. I daren't, for I have been that unruly son at times.

Faith in God is vital to us; if there is anything that has caused you to lose heart, then talk with God, talk with your loving Father... He is eager to listen and quick to love.

> My son, do not make light of the Lord's discipline, and do not lose heart when he rebukes you, because the Lord disciplines those he loves, and he punishes everyone he accepts as a son. (Hebrews 12:5b–6)

Keep Jesus as your inspiration

There is something in human nature that I have given much thought to lately.

When someone hurts us, why is it that we often take the pain out on our own self by abusing ourselves?

We drink too much, smoke too much, eat too much, take risks with sex, and even self-harm. We can let cleanliness go, we stop trusting and making friendships, and our lives begin to empty of any good we had in us when we take the pain out on ourselves... we lose heart.

I have been giving much thought to how Jesus dealt with hurt. You never see Him abusing Himself or others.

> **How did He endure such hardship and not lash out at others or Himself?**

Maybe it was because He knew without a shadow of doubt what His life on earth was to accomplish. The pain was part of the journey, and so He accepted it and spoke with His Father about it.

I had dinner with two friends last night. There is something that takes place when you are able to share your deepest hurts with one another... a healing.

People such as Sir Winston Churchill, Nelson Mandela, Billy Graham and Johnny Cash inspire me. These are just some of the men in history that encourage me to press on through my struggles and not let my hurts eat me away from the inside out.

But Jesus does more than inspire me – He travels with me by His Holy Spirit. I know I will never be perfect this side of heaven, but having the Spirit of God dwell in me gives me hope that I can allow Jesus to live through me.

We are created to love and love well, even if the storm is raging and our wounds are bleeding. Loving well is healing in itself.

I want to know Jesus, I want to follow Him, and I want to be like Him.

I have that potential when His Spirit is in me, and I have the heart to pursue my dream... even if the journey is filled with pain.

Don't lose heart by ignoring the Man, the Son, and the Saviour Jesus Christ.

A NEW WORLD

Chapter Ten: A New World

I believe that in all of us there is the need to do something of worth with the life we have been given. To be someone bigger and better than we are today, and to accomplish something that is much greater than ourselves.

I live with this desire daily. It's at times very uncomfortable, it's always challenging, and constantly forces me to look at myself and the way I live, think and understand why my emotions are what they are.

Like you, I was not created to live this life on my own. I have friends, family and acquaintances that I journey through each day with. We all have stories and experiences that stay with us because of the people they were created with.

I write this today having received the news that one of my STC (St Thomas Crookes) family members passed away last night unexpectedly. They were only in their forties. We don't have time to waste, our lives will come and go just as the generations before us and the ones that will follow.

If we are to impact our world and the one we all live in, then we must get involved in what is taking place on the main stage of history. We must put to rest the barking dog that says, 'We have little or nothing to offer and in what world could you ever make a significant change?'

> **I like to dance on my own,
> but it's much more fun dancing with others**

I have been moved deep within myself recently to find ways to make sure my faith impacts this world in ways that matter. We can all talk about Jesus and repeat His teachings, but it is another thing altogether to act upon them by giving people their dignity back.

I signed up to be added to ONE, the 'campaign to make poverty history' email list.

Below is a portion of e-news from ONE:

> It's being called the 'Silent Tsunami.' In three years, prices for the basic staples that feed the world – wheat, rice and corn – have risen by a staggering 83%. For people in the developing world, affording enough food to eat is becoming a daily struggle for survival.[5]

A daily struggle for survival... I know many who read this will struggle from month to month to make ends meet, but we sit in a centrally heated or air-conditioned home with access to the Internet, a fridge that holds food, running water, electricity and a cell phone.

But there are 100 million people around the world who have none of these comforts that we take for granted, and they face a deeper poverty because of the rise in basic food costs, and hundreds of thousands of these will confront famine and starvation.

I have a modern-day leprosy that eats away at me, numbing me to the pain of my brothers and sisters in other lands and leaving me focusing on myself. I fear I have become selfish, which is in complete contrast to the faith I profess.

As I mentioned in chapter five, one of my favourite films is *A Knight's Tale*, a moving tale of how a young peasant boy dreams of becoming a knight.

In this film there is a scene where Sir William (the peasant boy) has faked his records of nobility and entered a jousting contest, which only those of noble birth could enter.

As in many good films the main character, who stands for good, has an arch-enemy who stands for all that is unjust and wrong, and thrown into the mix is the heart of a beautiful woman who both have a desire to win.

Sir William comes in second to his arch-enemy, Adhemar, who with contempt turns to William and says, 'You have been weighed, you have been tested and you have been found wanting. In what world could you ever beat me?'

In what world could we ever beat poverty? In what world could I become so giving that selfishness is no longer my leprosy? In what world...

Maybe it's time to create a new world!

You will find it

'In what world could you ever be...'

Do you ever hear the voice that says that to you?

In what world could you ever graduate from college or university?

In what world could you ever find the right partner?

In what world could you ever have a job that is fulfilling?

In what world could you ever have children?

In what world could you ever be a writer?

In what world could you ever grow a 'come as you are' church'?

In what world could you ever get out of debt?

In what world could you ever learn to play that instrument?

In what world could you ever have your heart put back together?

In what world could you ever lose the weight?

In what world could you ever be unselfish?

In what world could you ever become the person you dream of becoming?

You and I are the same in that we hear the voice of the one who wants to keep us just where we are... selfish. More concerned about ourselves than others, taking for granted that we have a roof over our heads, food on the table and clothes to wear. Rarely giving a second thought to the poor around us, and even when we do, we find ourselves believing the voice saying, 'In what world could you ever make a difference?'

This is the voice of our arch-enemy, who has a number of names: Satan, Lucifer, the devil and Beelzebub; but no name is more fitting than this one: father of lies.

Why do we believe his lies? Does it make us feel better about ourselves if we don't believe we can make a difference in this world – then we won't feel guilty by sitting back and doing nothing?

I find myself today not wanting to sit back anymore. What does this mean? It scares me to think of the changes that would have to take place both within me and in my little world. Life would never be the same again, not for me and not for those whose lives I begin to touch.

I am reminded of something Jesus said: 'Whoever wants to save his life will lose it, but whoever loses his life for me and for the gospel will save it' (Mark 8:35; see also Matthew 16:25 Luke 9:24).

Will I only ever find true life by creating a new world, a new world in which I am abandoned to the compassion of God, a new world in which I have lost my life and am actually living out the gospel?

A new world, can this really be? Can I create a place where I am healed of this modern-day leprosy called selfishness? A world where religious robes, buildings and traditions mean nothing but the poor mean everything?

Is it my body that needs to be made new before the world around me can be changed, or is it my spirit, soul and mind?

Jesus came to earth as God in the flesh, a God-man. He created a new world; we can read about it in the New Testament. This new world is what I have been dreaming about, it is what calls to my heart. Like the 'One Ring' in *The Lord of the Rings*, my heart is trying to find its way back to its Maker.

> **If I am created in God's image,
> then I have the power to create, and so do you**

Like so many that have gone before us, we are to create the new world, the one in which we will no longer be content to listen to the father of lies and his untruths.

Jesus created a new world. He created a new you when you became His disciple. It is our call, our duty and our destiny to give ourselves to the Kingdom Come.

Let's explore... let's create this new world together.

> If you try to hang on to your life, you will lose it. But if you give up your life for my sake and for the sake of the Good News, you will save it. (Mark 8:35, NLT)

Create

Local governments look for opportunities to better the area they govern. One of the ways they do this is by building new environments for people to live in.

I have seen a number of projects/housing estates that have suffered from high crime rates, where the whole community has been rehoused so a regeneration programme can take place.

This is where homes, shops, workplaces and even schools are demolished and the whole area is redeveloped. New housing goes up, along with new shopping areas and places of education. The goal is to create a better environment than the one that previously existed.

In every human heart there is the need to 'do better'. To create a better life for ourselves and for those around us. Regeneration projects can only be accomplished when a number of hearts come together and with their passion to create a better world, they create one.

When you and I decided to follow Jesus, we became His disciples and His kingdom became our kingdom. The 'kingdom come, your [God's] will be done on earth as it is in heaven' (Matthew 6:10) started within us; we became new creations in Christ Jesus. A regeneration programme started in our soul, spirit and mind.

> **God the Father, God the Son and God the Holy Spirit got together and birthed a new world within us**

This then ignites with the image of God that you and I are created in. God is a creator and so the need to create is in us all. This results in our hearts being infused with the power of God, driving us to show this new world through our thoughts and ideas, words and plans, and actions.

The regeneration of the world around us starts in us and comes through us.

In what world could you ever beat poverty and negativity? In the new world which comes from experiencing a new birth.

We must travel into the unknown of God if we are to come out of this black hole. I know the task is massive. It was never meant to be met by the courage of just one heart, but of many hearts that have gone through the new birth, coming together with their passion to create a better world.

What name can we give to this group of hearts? God calls them the Church.

We can create a new world for only a few by acting on our own, but if we come together with the Creator as our King Arthur, then at the round table for equals we have the opportunity to create a new world for millions.

But if your experience of Church is anything like mine, you will have good church experiences and bad ones. I ask the question today, does the Church accomplish what God created her to do, or have we been believing the lie from the father of lies, 'In what world could you ever…?', falling into the trap and delusion that we can't do anything significant for the poor and needy, and so slip into a Church coma where we experience a painful death through the modern-day leprosy I call selfishness?

Is it time for us to create again?

Is it time for a new Church?

Is it time for us to give ourselves to the Trinity so that God can start a regeneration programme?

> So from now on we regard no-one from a worldly point of view. Though we once regarded Christ in this way, we do so no longer. Therefore, if anyone is in Christ, he is a new creation; the old has gone, the new has come! All this is from God, who reconciled us to himself through Christ and gave us the ministry of reconciliation ... (2 Corinthians 5:16–18)

The new world – a new Church

You don't have to be a rocket scientist to come to the conclusion that this generation in the Western world is dissatisfied with Church.

And don't kid yourself that it is only the young and the un-churched that carry such disappointment and discontent. Many who attend church week in week out have the same feelings and convictions, but are slowly dying in the coma.

I'm dissatisfied, but I refuse to stay this way. Like thousands on planet Earth, I have joined the search for simple Church, authentic, real and effective. Church that is more concerned about meeting needs than the presentation of the sermon.

Church that doesn't tell us what to think but allows us to explore and discover the age-old truths for ourselves... one that is a round table of equals.

I have been reading a book called *UnChristian* by David Kinnaman, which contains the results of research that has been done over a number of years into how those who don't go to church view the Church.

For want of better names for those who don't attend church, they call them 'outsiders', and those who do attend church, 'churchgoers'. A list of phrases were given to describe religious faith and those taking the survey had to indicate if they thought each phrase described present-day Christianity.

Here are the top three phrases that outsiders and churchgoers said best described present-day Christianity:

	Outsiders	Churchgoers
Anti homosexual	91%	80%
Judgemental	87%	52%
Hypocritical – saying one thing, doing another	85%	47%

In one sense it does not matter if these statistics are true. If they are people's perceptions of God's Church, then it's their reality, and if it's their reality, they will choose to stay far away.

I believe in the Church; it is the vehicle and body which God created to display His heart and power through. God is eager to show compassion and love, and He wants His life to flow through the thoughts and ideas, words and plans, and actions of His Church.

I don't have all the answers, but I do have a searching heart and a desire to be authentic and productive in my personal faith and in my church relationships. I recognise the need for change in the world, but change in the Church must come first, and for that to happen there must be a change in me.

You may be in a place where you feel spoiled to just attend church. It used to be comfortable and OK, but something has changed within you and contentment has flown away, leaving a searching and a struggle that you are not comfortable with.

Wrestle with God and don't let go. (Your walk is never the same after you wrestle with God).

I pray for you today as I pray for myself, as we wrestle and search for the ways in which the ancient truths are to be lived out in this day and age. I ask that you and I will find our place in the new world... the new world where the bride of Christ does not look like she has been in a car wreck, but where she is stunningly beautiful and ready for her wedding day.

May our search lead us into a life where God's truth is not tailored to make us look fashionable, but wrapped around us like an uncut garment, bringing healing to our lands.

The new world – welcome!

Earlier in this chapter I shared a moment from the film, *A Knight's Tale*, where William's enemy, Adhemar, tells him, after defeating him in a tournament, that he has been weighed and tested and found wanting... in what world could William ever beat him?

Do ever feel like your circumstances say to you that you have been weighed, tested and found wanting?

We can find ourselves in situations and circumstances that could easily keep us from ever moving on beyond the present time. They weigh us and test us and when we fail or feel overwhelmed, we begin to feel too small, weak or insignificant to rise up and meet the challenge... we find ourselves wanting.

Wanting and needing, searching for strength, wisdom, peace, hope and help. We know we are not up to the challenge that has arrived on our doorstep... we need an answer.

So we dream about a solution, a magic formula, but none seem to be the magic that you need to turn the tide.

I believe that is how many churches are; they are stuck in the busy programmes they run. All those attending feel they are living free and not wanting, but in reality they are all just busy, sleeping in a coma, ignoring the dead elephant in the middle of the room that is a reminder that everything is not OK.

Often when we face the reality that everything is not OK, that we have not created a world in which we are greater than our enemy, we just create another programme that keeps Jesus' followers away from the un-churched and entrenched in the Church bubble.

If we, the Church, were to be weighed and tested in respect to how we reach the poor, needy and un-churched, would we be found wanting?

The great news, the gospel of our Lord Jesus Christ, the hope we have, is that the Creator of the Church dwells in us once we decide to follow Jesus.

The answer we are looking for is not found in a programme but in a person. If only we really would allow ourselves to be guided by the Holy Spirit, then we would not only surprise those we come into contact with but we would surprise ourselves.

We would find ourselves in places that we have been avoiding, spending time with people that are outsiders, giving our stuff away – and while experiencing all this, the Word of God that we have read and listened to month in, month out, would all of a sudden make sense as it came alive within.

At the end of *A Knight's Tale*, Sir William beats his enemy, Adhemar, and while he lies there defeated on the ground, Sir William and his friends lean over him saying, 'You have been weighed, you have been tested and you have been found wanting... welcome to the new world!'

If we can go on the journey and allow God by His Holy Spirit to transform us into the image of Christ, we too will be able to say to our enemy 'welcome to the new world' as we simply act out of God's love and compassion.

After all, 'greater is he that is in you than he that is in the world' (1 John 4:4, ASV).

When Jesus rose from the grave, He invited us to the new world...

Have you taken up His invitation?

> You, dear children, are from God and have overcome them, because the one who is in you is greater than the one who is in the world. (1 John 4:4)

End Notes

1. 'The Darkest Places', MxPx, from the album *Panic*, SideOneDummy Records. Permission granted by Mike Herrera.

2. Desmond Tutu, *God Has a Dream* (London: Rider, 2005).

3. *King Arthur,* Touchstone Pictures (presents), Jerry Bruckheimer Films (presents), Green Hills Productions (co-production), World 2000 Entertainment (co-production).

4. *A Knight's Tale* (2001) Columbia Pictures Corporation (presents) (as Columbia Pictures), Escape Artists, Finestkind, Black and Blu Entertainment.

5. www.one.org

6. David Kinnaman, *UnChristian* (Grand Rapids, MI: Baker Books, 2012).